Jewish History: A Very Short Introduction

VERY SHORT INTRODUCTIONS are for anyone wanting a stimulating and accessible way into a new subject. They are written by experts, and have been translated into more than 45 different languages.

The series began in 1995, and now covers a wide variety of topics in every discipline. The VSI library now contains over 526 volumes—a Very Short Introduction to everything from Psychology and Philosophy of Science to American History and Relativity—and continues to grow in every subject area.

Very Short Introductions available now:

ACCOUNTING Christopher Nobes
ADOLESCENCE Peter K. Smith
ADVERTISING Winston Fletcher
AFRICAN AMERICAN RELIGION
    Eddie S. Glaude Jr
AFRICAN HISTORY
    John Parker and Richard Rathbone
AFRICAN RELIGIONS
    Jacob K. Olupona
AGEING Nancy A. Pachana
AGNOSTICISM Robin Le Poidevin
AGRICULTURE Paul Brassley and
    Richard Soffe
ALEXANDER THE GREAT
    Hugh Bowden
ALGEBRA Peter M. Higgins
AMERICAN HISTORY Paul S. Boyer
AMERICAN IMMIGRATION
    David A. Gerber
AMERICAN LEGAL HISTORY
    G. Edward White
AMERICAN POLITICAL HISTORY
    Donald Critchlow
AMERICAN POLITICAL PARTIES
    AND ELECTIONS L. Sandy Maisel
AMERICAN POLITICS
    Richard M. Valelly
THE AMERICAN PRESIDENCY
    Charles O. Jones
THE AMERICAN REVOLUTION
    Robert J. Allison
AMERICAN SLAVERY
    Heather Andrea Williams
THE AMERICAN WEST Stephen Aron

AMERICAN WOMEN'S HISTORY
    Susan Ware
ANAESTHESIA Aidan O'Donnell
ANARCHISM Colin Ward
ANCIENT ASSYRIA Karen Radner
ANCIENT EGYPT Ian Shaw
ANCIENT EGYPTIAN ART AND
    ARCHITECTURE Christina Riggs
ANCIENT GREECE Paul Cartledge
THE ANCIENT NEAR EAST
    Amanda H. Podany
ANCIENT PHILOSOPHY Julia Annas
ANCIENT WARFARE Harry Sidebottom
ANGELS David Albert Jones
ANGLICANISM Mark Chapman
THE ANGLO-SAXON AGE John Blair
ANIMAL BEHAVIOUR
    Tristram D. Wyatt
THE ANIMAL KINGDOM
    Peter Holland
ANIMAL RIGHTS David DeGrazia
THE ANTARCTIC Klaus Dodds
ANTISEMITISM Steven Beller
ANXIETY Daniel Freeman and
    Jason Freeman
THE APOCRYPHAL GOSPELS
    Paul Foster
ARCHAEOLOGY Paul Bahn
ARCHITECTURE
    Andrew Ballantyne
ARISTOCRACY William Doyle
ARISTOTLE Jonathan Barnes
ART HISTORY Dana Arnold
ART THEORY Cynthia Freeland

WILLIAM SHAKESPEARE
Stanley Wells
WITCHCRAFT Malcolm Gaskill
WITTGENSTEIN A. C. Grayling
WORK Stephen Fineman
WORLD MUSIC Philip Bohlman

THE WORLD TRADE
ORGANIZATION Amrita Narlikar
WORLD WAR II Gerhard L. Weinberg
WRITING AND SCRIPT
Andrew Robinson
ZIONISM Michael Stanislawski

Available soon:

BRANDING Robert Jones
POVERTY Philip N. Jefferson
PAIN Rob Boddice

MULTILINGUALISM John C. Maher
OCEANS Dorrik Stow

For more information visit our web site

www.oup.com/vsi/

David N. Myers

JEWISH HISTORY

A Very Short Introduction

OXFORD
UNIVERSITY PRESS

OXFORD

UNIVERSITY PRESS

Oxford University Press is a department of the University of Oxford.
It furthers the University's objective of excellence in research, scholarship,
and education by publishing worldwide. Oxford is a registered trade mark of
Oxford University Press in the UK and certain other countries.

Published in the United States of America by Oxford University Press
198 Madison Avenue, New York, NY 10016, United States of America.

Library of Congress Cataloging-in-Publication Data
Names: Myers, David N., author.
Title: Jewish history : a very short introduction / David N. Myers.
Description: Oxford ; New York : Oxford University Press, [2017] |
Includes bibliographical references and index.
Identifiers: LCCN 2016047943 | ISBN 9780199730988 (pbk. : alk. paper)
Subjects: LCSH: Jews—History.
Classification: LCC DS117 .M94 2017 |
DDC 909/.04924—dc23 LC record
available at https://lccn.loc.gov/2016047943

Printed by Integrated Books International, United States of America

To Yosef Hayim Yerushalmi z"l

Contents

List of illustrations

Acknowledgments

Attempting to write a history as long as that of the Jews in such a short space is a challenging task. I would not have been able to do so without the incisive comments and careful reading of friends and colleagues. I extend my deep thanks to Sarah Abrevaya Stein, Michael Berenbaum, John Efron, David Ruderman, Ra'anan Boustan, and Nomi Stolzenberg. Seth Schwartz, Jonathan Ray, Benjamin Gampel, and Aryeh Cohen provided helpful input at crucial points in the process. A special debt of appreciation goes to Jonathan Elukin, who undertook an exhaustive critical reading of the manuscript as a reader for Oxford University Press and improved it considerably.

Nancy Toff models the intellectual seriousness, attention to detail, and sense of humor that make for a great editor. She has been saintly in her patience in waiting for this book. Elda Granata, assistant history editor at Oxford University Press, answered every query, large and small, with great efficiency. My thanks as well to Shina Harshavardhan, Talia Graff, and Paul State who provided expert support in the copy-editing process.

Finally, I dedicate this book to Yosef Hayim Yerushalmi (1932–2009). My encounter with him at Columbia University in 1985 altered my life, transforming the study of Jewish history into the most exciting intellectual pursuit imaginable. That it has remained so to this day is an ongoing testament to the power of Yosef Yerushalmi's example as scholar and teacher. It was his insistence on studying the entire course of Jewish history that has enabled this book.

Introduction

"Why have Jews survived through the ages while other civilizations and religions have come and gone?" Thus begins the online "Ask the Rabbi" Web page sponsored by Chabad, one of the most prominent and active Orthodox groups in the world. The response delivered by Rabbi Moshe Goldman, a Chabad emissary in Canada, is not surprising: "G-d did it and continues to do it."

The rabbi's answer rests on the claim that Jews are God's Chosen People and thus guaranteed a special form of divine protection. This assertion is deeply rooted in Jewish history and figures prominently in the Hebrew Bible and many other traditional Jewish writings. The Book of Genesis reports on the "everlasting covenant" that God forged with Abraham and his descendants. Later the medieval and early modern Jewish mystics referred to the Jewish people as "netsah Yisra'el," the eternal Israel that would survive all earthly travails.

This traditional claim does not lend itself to sustained historical inquiry into how exactly the Jews survived. Indeed, we still struggle to understand what explains the endurance of this small people, when so many other larger and more powerful groups— great world empires from the Romans to the Mongols to the Ottomans—have passed from the stage of history.

Complicating the query are two recurrent characteristics in the annals of the Jews. First, throughout history, they have been a people in movement, beginning with the mythic account of the sojourn of their founding patriarch Abraham from Ur (in present-day Iraq) to the land of Canaan some four thousand years ago. They have never ceased moving throughout their history and have made their ways to all corners of the globe, from Yemen to the Netherlands to Brazil to Australia; in fact, they pioneered the very notion of a "diaspora," a Greek term invented to describe their dispersed state. One scholar has labeled Jews the classic "Mercurians" in the world, alluding to their constant mobility and resourcefulness in adapting to new settings.

Along with the Jews' constant motion throughout their long and wide dispersion, there is a second striking feature of their history: they have consistently been disliked. The long history of antisemitism—a modern term applied anachronistically to an old phenomenon—has few peers. For thousands of years, Jews have been subject to stigmatization, marginalization, and full-blown attempts at elimination. Perhaps no group in human history has been regarded with such disdain for so long by so many. What is especially remarkable is the malleability of the phenomenon. Jews have been hated as jealous Christ-killers and godless atheists, rootless cosmopolitans and insular ghetto dwellers, internationalist communists and arch-capitalists.

And yet, they have survived. They have repeatedly defied the odds by overcoming challenge, crisis, and tragedy with new forms of religious, cultural, and political expressions. Tellingly, in the wake of the most sustained attempt to eradicate them during the Holocaust, they have developed two of the largest and, by many measures, most successful communities produced during their long journey: Israel and the United States.

Their resilience has reduced even avowedly secular observers to mystical reverie. The early-twentieth-century historian Simon Dubnow, one of the three towering Jewish historians of the modern age (along with Heinrich Graetz and Salo W. Baron), wrote of the "secret of the existence" of the Jews. Despite his own abandonment of religious belief as an adolescent, he echoed the explanation of traditionalists for whom Jewish survival was a supernatural miracle.

The veil of mystery has inspired many explanations. Apart from the traditional biblical view that Jews are God's Chosen People, they range from the assertion of Church Fathers in the fourth century that the Jews were preserved, albeit in a debased state, in order to bear witness to the truth of Christianity to Hannah Arendt's notion in the twentieth century that it was the alliance of Jews with political sovereigns that saved them—until the rise of the Nazis, when it proved to be their undoing. More recently, scholars have argued that it was the premium placed on literacy in the post–Second Temple era that provided Jews with a competitive advantage that enabled them to survive.

Amidst the welter of explanations, this book pursues a different tack, seeking to explain how, rather than why, the Jews have survived. It does so as part of the effort to chronicle, in a very short space, the long history of the Jews, for their very survival is the main drama in that tale. We begin by recalling what evolutionary biologists teach us, namely, that human survival writ large has been enabled by the capacity to respond and adapt to a variety of challenging environments, not just one.

The Jews are an especially illuminating case study of this proposition, having weathered frequent challenges by developing a mechanism that allowed them to adapt to new environments without losing a distinctive sense of cultural self. Ironically, the two factors mentioned above—the constant mobility of Jews and the persistent hostility toward them—have been key components of that adaptive mechanism.

This seems curious, if not delusional. How could it be, for example, that the enmity that Jews have faced throughout their history could preserve them? Drawing on the Roman historian

Introduction (side margin)

Tacitus, the seventeenth-century renegade Jewish philosopher Benedictus Spinoza wrote that the stubborn adherence of the ancient Jews to their particular laws led them to separate from their Gentile neighbors. This segregation made them alien and despised in the eyes of the Gentiles. Far from leading to their disappearance, Spinoza argued, it was "Gentile hatred" that preserved the Jews. On his provocative reading, it was not just the external barriers posed by Gentile society that kept the Jews apart. It was also the Jews' own consciousness of being reviled that fortified their sense of being distinct. This dynamic took on curious new form in the post-Enlightenment era, when Jews began to lose the high degree of faith and commitment to ritual observance of their medieval predecessors. In the absence of those pillars, Gentile enmity—and the organized fight against it— became central modes of Jewish identity. Spinoza's insight holds true up to today; both antisemitism and the efforts to combat it define how Jews see and define themselves.

But there are obvious constraints on the surprising logic of hatred as a preservative force. When hatred leads to mass murder, as in the Holocaust, then it destroys rather than preserves. But throughout much of their history, Jews were disliked in ways that reinforced their sense of being a distinct people. Seen in isolation, this perspective risks reducing Jewish history to an unrelentingly "lachrymose," or tearful view, to borrow the memorable phrase of Salo Baron. But Jewish history is far more than the static tale of antisemitism.

It is also a story of constant motion that kept Jews lithe on their feet, moving from place to place when the need arose, like a good boxer (of which there were more than a few Jews) who is able to dodge and deflect the full brunt of blows directed against him. The ceaseless mobility of the Jews led to a second key factor in enabling their survival—what we may call in shorthand "assimilation" (otherwise known as "acculturation"). In contemporary parlance, this word induces panic in Jewish community officials, who point to high intermarriage rates and weakening organizational affiliation as signs of the impending disappearance of the Jews. In historical terms, assimilation refers to the process by which Jews, in making their way to new locales, absorbed the linguistic and cultural norms of their Gentile neighbors—and then shared their own. This peculiar understanding follows the usage of historian Gerson Cohen, who argued in 1966 that assimilation as a means of cultural interaction was not only unavoidable in Jewish history, but also *necessary* to the survival of the Jews. Without the constant cultural encounters, enacted every day over the course of millennia, Jews would have become fossilized, as the British historian Arnold Toynbee famously and mistakenly claimed they had. In fact, it was the interaction with non-Jews that allowed for the explosive diversity of Jewish culture and the ongoing vitality of its practitioners.

An instructive example of this process is the range of Jewish languages that Jews developed apart from Hebrew, beginning with Aramaic and Greek in antiquity and extending to Judeo-Arabic, Judeo-Persian, Judeo-Italian, Judeo-Spanish (Ladino), and Yiddish, among many others. These languages emerged out of the daily exchange that Jews had with Gentile neighbors and the vernacular they spoke. Prior to modern times, Jews typically acquired fluency in the tongues of their host societies, but they still felt a need to create their own encoded version of them, accessible only to other Jews. In most instances, they did so by transcribing the language not in vernacular script but in Hebrew letters, while at the same time adding Hebrew words to the linguistic mix. What resulted was a rich and entwined bilingualism, whereby Jews spoke and wrote both in the vernacular and in the Hebraized cognate. Out of this web emerged great works of cultural production—legal tomes in Aramaic, philosophy in Judeo-Arabic, biblical commentary in Judeo-Spanish, and *belles lettres* in Yiddish.

This kind of cultural work reflects not only the potential, but also the limits of Jewish "assimilation." Jews were able to tone their cultural muscles as they balanced between adaptation to the broader world and preservation of the borders of their narrower Jewish community. Maintaining this balance was not simply a matter of Jewish will. It also depended on a wide range of external conditions, including, most especially, the persistence of antisemitism.

It is at this point that the two key factors converge. Assimilation, understood in the idiosyncratic sense above, ensured ongoing cultural vitality, allowing Jews to survive for millennia in a variety of settings beyond their homeland. Antisemitism, meanwhile, guaranteed that the path of Jews to full integration was frequently blocked. Unlikely as it may seem, these two forces have interacted, allowing Jews to persist, when many other groups faded.

In following this fascinating story, I have opted not to divide the book in conventional fashion, namely into chronologically based chapters. Instead, I have chosen five themes to capture some of the major animating forces of the Jewish past. Each of these themes is rendered in the plural; thus, "Culture" is not employed but rather "Cultures" to reflect the diversity of cultural encounters of a widely dispersed group in many different venues. The five themes are meant to be representative but by no means exhaustive. At the same time, they are intended to be interwoven and cumulative, as well as occasionally overlapping to reinforce points of particular import.

Invariably in an undertaking of this sort in which selectivity and distillation are key, not all major categories of historical experience that deserve attention—for example, economics—can be included. It is my hope that, notwithstanding this and other deficiencies, the reader will gain a rich enough sense of the flowing currents of the Jewish past to grasp its intrigue and, even, its marvel.

Chapter 1
Names

"What's in a name? That which we call a rose by any other name would smell as sweet." This memorable line uttered by Juliet to Romeo reminds us that people, like the thing we call a rose, have an essence beyond the names we use for them. One thinks of this in the case of the Jews who have assumed several names over the course of their collective life, including but hardly restricted to the term "Jews."

Alongside this designation the group was known in antiquity by a number of other names: Israelites, Hebrews, Judeans, and Judahites. In later periods, they became subdivided into different categories with distinct names including Samaritans, Karaites, Rabbanites, Ashkenazim, Sephardim, and Mizrahim. The shifting names remind us of the dynamism of the Jewish past. In appraising the religious tradition that emerged out of it, the great twentieth-century scholar Gershom Scholem once declared that Judaism was marked by the fact that it had no single essence to it. How then might we conjure up a stable image of Jewish history if the religion that anchors it has no essence? We might conceive of it as a great and well-excavated archaeological site: accretions of culture are layered on top of one another, each of which represents a different spirit of the time. Seen as a whole, the site conveys the image of a highly sophisticated and evolving civilization.

This image, helpful as it may be, has real limits, for it suggests a single site in which the group was born and reached maturity. But the Jews were, for much of their existence, a diaspora people. Accordingly, we have to modify our guiding image of Jewish history to include multiple sites scattered over time and place, enabling a wide array of cultural expressions but at the same time mandating the cultivation of an ongoing network of communication and mutual aid.

This web of connected sites prompts us to speak not of one unvarying Jewish identity, but rather of connected "identities" that bridge the experience of Jews over time and place. The link between these identities is not mere ancient mythology nor the invention of modern ideologues, imposed, as some have argued, to justify latter-day politics. There are long-standing beliefs, rituals, kinship ties, and an historical consciousness that have lent a deep sense of a common fate and experience to Jews. The task ahead is to understand the different, though connected, ways in which Jews have chosen to identify themselves. In so doing, we can see the continuity and change that add such animating tension to Jewish history.

Tribe

In jocular parlance today, Jews often refer to one another as "members of the tribe" (MOTs). The term serves as code to establish an affinity between two people who otherwise bear no visible trace of their Jewishness. To be sure, the absence of discernable markers is a new phenomenon, but the assertion of a Jewish tribal bond has deep historical roots. Indeed, as Jews came into being as a collective thousands of years ago, they, or their precursors, organized themselves according to tribal patterns.

But when exactly did that occur? The difficulty is not merely that the Jews did not announce their entry onto the stage of history with a grand proclamation. Even more confounding, we don't really know when the story begins. The traditional explanation places the starting point sometime around 2000–1900 BCE and revolves around the figure of Abraham, the founding patriarch of the Israelite religion.

According to the traditional account, Abraham, or Abram as he was then known, left his home in Ur in southern Mesopotamia for the land of Canaan at God's behest. Alas, the only evidence of Abraham's existence—or for that matter of his heirs, Isaac and Jacob—is in the Hebrew Bible, making it difficult to corroborate.

Scholars have also puzzled over the next major chapter in the received biblical narrative—the story of the flight to Egypt to escape famine in the land of Canaan by the children of Jacob, or Israel, as he was renamed. The children of Israel, the Bible tells us in the Book of Exodus, fell into servitude to Egyptian pharaohs, but were led to liberation by the greatest prophet of the Israelite religion, Moses. It was Moses who decisively separated himself and his followers from the regnant polytheism of the ancient Near East by declaring belief in one God. And it was he, the tradition tells us, who guided his people across the Red Sea into freedom in the Sinai Desert.

But again, we lack basic extra-biblical evidence that could attest to the existence of the Israelites and Moses in Egypt and, more particularly, to their flight to freedom. Even without overwhelming external evidence, the Israelites' tale of Exodus has had deep resonances beyond the Jews, becoming one of the most widely replicated and admired narratives of liberation from oppression.

What we do possess is an important piece of external evidence from the thirteenth century BCE that makes explicit reference to "Israel." It is the Merneptah stele, a stone inscription that describes, in verse, the triumph of an Egyptian king, Merneptah, over a number of groups in the land of Canaan. The final line

Names

relates: "Israel is laid waste, his seed is not." It is not clear what battle the stele is describing, but it seems to be referring not to a place name but to an ethnic group. Indeed, we begin to pick up the trail of a group or groups associated with that name in the thirteenth century, when Egyptian imperial control over the land was beginning to wane. Neither a unified social cohort nor an established polity existed at this point, but rather a network of nomadic tribes, which may have been divided according to the sons of Jacob—otherwise known as the *bene Yisra'el*, the children of Israel. (The names of the twelve tribes are Reuben, Simeon, Levi, Judah, Zebulon, Issachar, Dan, Gad, Asher, Naphtali, Joseph, and Benjamin.)

The Bible is replete with references to the distinct tribes; the Book of Joshua, for example, offers a detailed description of the disparate tribes joining forces to regain the land of Canaan, which God had promised them. Whether they consolidated themselves outside of Canaan or molded their distinct tribal identities within, we do not know. But it is reasonable to assume that between the thirteenth and eleventh centuries BCE, residents could be found in the central mountain region of Canaan who shared a number of key properties that identify them as precursors to today's Jews:

- **Family**: The most basic unit of social organization for the Israelite tribes was the tight-knit family with its own land presided over by the head male figure, father or grandfather, from whom identity was transmitted at this point.

- **Genealogy**: Members of families traced their own histories back several generations and linked their particular stories to the wanderings of the children of Israel. This became the foundation for Israelite historical consciousness.

- **Language**: Israelite tribes of Canaan spoke an indigenous Semitic language that would later be referred to as *Yehudit* and which we call today Hebrew. The formation of this language reveals the extent to which its speakers belonged to the larger Canaanite cultural world of the day.

4

Little concrete evidence exists of a fully developed religious system by this point, apart from the Bible. The Book of Exodus makes reference to a portable Ark of the Covenant that the tribes brought with them from Mt. Sinai that contained the Ten Commandments. This terse set of prescriptions would become one of the Israelites' most notable contributions to the world—a moral code that has anchored both religious and political systems ever since. One of the Commandments declared that they should worship no other god than the God of Israel. But when exactly to date the advent of this important development—the rise of the monotheistic faith in a single god—remains an open question. Some scholars trace the idea to the preceding Egyptian period. Others date it centuries later, noting that the tribes continued to worship a variety of local gods such as El, Asherah, and Baal, only gradually developing the conviction in the supreme power of a god known by the letters YHWH. Even at this early stage, we can imagine a process by which the Israelites remolded local practices and ideas with which they were intimately familiar into their own distinctive forms.

Meanwhile, the process of political consolidation of the tribes continued. An important step forward was the introduction of kingship into Israelite life at the end of the eleventh century in the person of Saul. Saul's ascent resulted from the desire for more stable leadership, as well as from a degree of borrowing from surrounding cultures (including the enemy Philistines).

Although some archaeologists have questioned the pace and scale of the next set of developments, it is reasonable to assume that Saul's successors, David and Solomon, took two key steps in the tenth century that would leave an indelible imprint on subsequent Jewish history: the creation by King David of a capital for the Israelite tribes in the city known as Jerusalem; and the construction by his son, Solomon, in the mid-tenth century of a Holy Temple, home to worship of the God of Israel and the Ten Commandments, and presided over by a priestly

1. Two kingdoms, the northern kingdom of Israel and the southern kingdom of Judah, had been united under King Solomon in the tenth century BCE, but split apart under his son Rehoboam. This division rendered them vulnerable to attack, as when the Assyrians laid siege to Israel in the late eighth century and the Babylonians to Judah in the early sixth century BCE.

class known as the *kohanim* who oversaw the preeminent ritual act of animal sacrifice. What is less clear—and serves to divide "maximalist" archaeologists from "minimalists"—is whether Jerusalem was the capacious capital of a powerful united kingdom created by David and Solomon or a provincial town of a small principality hovering nervously in the shadow of the stronger Philistines.

Regardless, the Holy Temple became the major religious institution in Israelite and later Jewish life—and a central focus of religious identity; even today, the aspiration to rebuild the Temple remains a feature of Jewish messianic speculation and planning. And yet, the presence of the Temple did not guarantee unity among the tribes. Not long after its erection, the northern tribes rebelled against the rule of Solomon's son Rehoboam leading to division into two entities, the northern kingdom of Israel and the southern kingdom of Judah, with Jerusalem at its center. The tensions between the two kingdoms, drawing in part on old tribal rivalries, created openings for regional powers intent on gaining power over the land of Canaan. The Assyrians attacked and laid waste to the northern kingdom in the late eighth century, followed in the sixth century by the assault of the upstart Babylonians under King Nebuchadnezzar on Judah. In the midst of that later attack in 587–586 BCE, Jerusalem and the Holy Temple were destroyed.

People of the Book

The assault on Jerusalem upended Israelite life in the city, with thousands of residents being sent into exile in Babylonia. Indeed, the very idea of "exile," indicating a state of physical and theological displacement (from God), received early and clear expression here. The prophet Jeremiah was particularly sharp in suggesting that the misfortune of the Jews, as they would come to be known in the sixth century BCE, was the result of their own sin in not heeding God's word.

An important question arises: with their capital city captured and their central religious institution destroyed, how did the exiles manage to survive? What held them together in this moment of crisis? Were it not for the mechanism of cultural adaptation that the exiles developed in Babylonia, they would have been long forgotten to history. This mechanism enabled them to absorb key features of Babylonian—and soon thereafter, Persian—culture such as language, names, dress styles, and culinary habits, as well as mythological and legal influences.

Significantly, their "assimilation" did not prevent the exiles from maintaining a deep connection to their ritual and theological roots. But it did mandate that they reimagine their religious experience beyond the institution of the Holy Temple, which no longer existed. Facing this new challenge, the exiles learned to balance between the degree of integration necessary to survive and adherence to Jewish cultic practices and beliefs. Out of this balancing act came innovation, including, some suggest, regular meetings to read and hear sacred texts on the Sabbath.

In 538 BCE, Cyrus the Persian conquered Babylonia and liberated the exiles. He also permitted the rebuilding of the Temple in 520, a date that inaugurates the Second Temple period in Jewish history. From this point forward, the group once known as Israelites may have been designated as "Jews," a term drawn from the Greek term "Ioudaios" whose origins are in the Hebrew "yehudi." For those in Jerusalem and its environs, the rebuilt Temple became again an important site of sacrifice overseen by priests. And yet, it was by no means the only such site in Palestine and abroad. As had been the case with the previous Temple, Jews who were unable or even unwilling to come from distant parts to Jerusalem practiced sacrifice in their own locales. Several hundred years later, in the third century, the first evidence emerges of institutions in which a new form of devotion—prayer—appears. These sites where prayer was practiced were called "synagogues" (Greek for assembly).

The Second Temple period abounded with religious innovation of many kinds, including the site and nature of devotion, as well as the evolution of the oral and written traditions that came to be known as the Torah, or the Hebrew Bible. Regarding its origins, a stark divergence exists in perspectives today between traditionalists who believe as an incontrovertible fact that the Torah was the product of Moses's receiving the word of God at Mt. Sinai and those who believe that it was the result of multiple human authors writing at different junctures in history. The latter view, held by most modern scholars, dates an early version known as the "Torat Moshe" (the Torah of Moses) to the Persian period (6th–5th centuries BCE). The fuller text, it is suggested, was likely not completed until the second century BCE.

At the core of Jewish biblical scripture are the Five Books of Moses (Genesis, Exodus, Leviticus, Numbers, and Deuteronomy); these books are complemented by nineteen books of prophetic and other writings to round out the Hebrew Bible. The centuries-long process of redaction of the various strands of the various books required extensive study, commentary, and reverence. Only gradually did it gain coherence and the veil of sanctity that envelops the Bible as sacred scripture. Once it achieved that state, the Hebrew Bible became a, if not the, central pillar of identity for Jews both within and outside the homeland.

At the same time, *study* of the holy text became a central preoccupation of Jewish culture, confined not only to experts, but also open to and expected of all Jewish men—and, in more recent times, available to women as well. The sacred text became, as one modern observer noted, a "portable fatherland" for the Jews, especially when there was no Temple standing or when Jews lived far away from the Temple. The primacy placed on scriptural study fueled, in turn, a powerful drive toward literacy, chiefly but not exclusively in Jewish languages. This literacy offered Jews a competitive advantage over less literate non-Jews in assuming skilled occupations in urban settings. It also inculcated in them a certain obsession with textual interpretation that generated many thousands of books—and more broadly, a rich culture of bookishness that would later lend to Jews the moniker "People of the Book." (The term actually was a translation of the Arabic "Ahl al-Kitāb" a name that medieval Muslims used for followers of monotheism who were devoted followers of the "Book," that is, the Bible.)

The bookishness of the Jews became a sore point for later Zionists, the Jewish nationalists who sought to leave behind the diaspora and return to the Promised Land. They aimed to replace what they saw as the excessively cerebral and passive diaspora Jew with a strong and brave "New Hebrew" rooted in the soil of the homeland. Notwithstanding their effort, the association between Jews and books has been virtually unbreakable. It has not only yielded a high rate of literacy among Jews, but also given rise to a wide range of achievements in the sciences, arts, and literature that has few precedents for a group the size of the Jews. One telling indicator of that range is the fact that Jews, while representing .2 percent of the world's population, have been awarded 22 percent of the Nobel Prizes in the world.

Diaspora people

From the time of the Babylonian conquest, Jews increasingly found themselves under the control of rulers beyond their homeland. The arrival of the Greeks in the Middle East, when Alexander the Great conquered the region beginning in 334 BCE, not only introduced a new major culture to the region; it also gave Jews a language to describe their existence outside of Palestine. Instead of "exile," with all its severe theological connotations, Jews outside the land of Israel dwelt now in the "diaspora," a less freighted Greek word connoting a scattered population. In the Greek diaspora, Jews became adept at balancing between their religious practices and the culture of their hosts. An illuminating case in point was Philo of Alexandria (25 BCE–50 CE), who mixed his vocation as a philosopher with a deep commitment to Jewish faith and practice. Drawing on both legacies, though writing in Greek, Philo set out to transform Jewish religion from a primal cult with a decidedly human-like God into a sophisticated belief system anchored by the notion of a vastly transcendent divine force. Although recognized today for his skillful integration of Jewish and Hellenistic values, Philo was ignored by the rabbis who emerged after the destruction of the Second Temple in Jerusalem by Roman forces in 70 CE.

That monumental event is often seen as the decisive beginning of Jewish dispersion lasting until the advent of the modern State of Israel in 1948. In fact, Jews had lived outside the land of Israel for centuries; and contrary to common assumption, they were not summarily dispatched from it in the year 70. By that point, they had developed mechanisms of adaptation that allowed them to shift from society to society, absorbing language, culture, and social habits necessary for survival while preserving their loyalty to Jewish religious law which would come to be known as *halakhah* (the way or path). Of course, not all desired or were able to maintain perfect equipoise; many Jews, over the course of centuries, found it easier to surrender the heavy demands of *halakhah* and embrace the surrounding culture and religion completely.

If the destruction of the Second Temple did not lead to the immediate or massive displacement of Jews, its effect over time was to decenter Jewish life away from the land of Israel even further. Jews mourned the loss of their Temple and articulated the desire to return to the homeland in their daily liturgy. At the same time, they found themselves at an ever greater physical and emotional remove from their homeland. They had been settled in Babylonia and Egypt for centuries. Under the arc of the Roman Empire, which succeeded the Greeks as the overlord of Palestine in the second century BCE, Jews fanned out from the Middle East to Europe, settling in Greece (Macedonia), Spain (Hispania), France (Gaul), and Italy as early as the first century BCE.

2. The Arch of Titus was built on the Via Sacra near the Roman Forum by the Emperor Domitian in honor of his brother, Titus, the general who led the Romans to victory over the Jews in Palestine in 70 CE. This portion of the arch depicts the plundering of the spoils of the Holy Temple. The destruction of the Temple, here celebrated by the Romans, has been a source of bitter sorrow for Jews over the centuries.

It was in the Roman period that an important new criterion of Jewishness emerged. Previously, it had been the father who determined the identity of his children as Jews. From this point forward, it was the mother, whose connection to her progeny could be readily verified via childbirth. For thousands of years until quite recently, Jewish mothers served as the sole validators of the Jewish identity of their children. More widely, women have played an important role as transmitters of Jewish identity throughout history by passing on ritual and social habits to their children in the confines of their homes. That said, women have often been placed in a subordinate status by virtue of the fact that Jewish law exempts them from performing all the ritual commandments incumbent on men. As a result of that distinction, it was men who dominated in the public sphere, whether in the Temple, synagogue, or marketplace.

There were, of course, exceptions to this rule. Examples included Deborah the Judge, who was reputed to be a courageous political and military leader in the 12th–11th centuries BCE, and the legendary Hannah, who was said to have refused to submit to her Greek persecutors in the second century BCE, choosing the path of martyrdom over apostasy and encouraging her seven sons to do the same. Later in the Middle Ages, women broke into the public domain in various limited ways. In Muslim lands, while largely confined to the home, women nonetheless appeared in court to represent their interests, in some settings, as frequently as men; and they did so in both Muslim and Jewish jurisdictions. Meanwhile, in Christian Europe, women, buoyed by a new ban on polygamy and related matters around 1000 CE, began to assert their rights more forthrightly in the region of northern France and Germany known as *Askhenaz*. Not only were they protected against indiscriminate divorce proceedings from their husbands; sources also attest to the fact that they played an active role in various businesses, including money-lending.

These innovations were forged in the midst of the *kehilah*, the autonomous Jewish communal body, which assumed a particularly developed state in *Askhenaz*. Communal life there revolved around scrupulous observance and study of Jewish law; leading scholars such as Rabbenu Gershom, known as "The Light of the Diaspora" and author of the ban on polygamy, endeavored to erect ordinances to assure piety and fairness within the community. The *kehilah* also had a set of lay leaders known as "the good men of the city" (*tov'e ha-`ir*) who regulated the economic life of the community, with a particular desire to safeguard the interests of locals at the expense of out-of-towners. A key challenge in this setting was how to navigate between the benefits of economic and, to an extent, social interaction with the larger Gentile community and the desire to preserve a measure of separation from it. On one hand, Jews had active commercial ties with Christians, often lived on the same streets, served as physicians to Christian clergy and rulers, and even taught Bible, Hebrew, and other subjects to Christians. On the other hand, a deep undercurrent of hostility between Jews and Christians stemmed back to the late Second Temple period and succeeding centuries. In the Middle Ages, this hostility persisted, but it prevented neither regular contact between the two groups nor the outbreak of periodic acts of violence by Christians against Jews.

One of the chief limiting factors on more persistent and lethal forms of violence was the protection afforded by local rulers through legal charters to the Jews, in which they were guaranteed physical security in exchange for providing important economic functions to the realm (e.g., as tax collectors, money lenders, or liquor purveyors). This arrangement harked back to the ancient doctrine of *dina di-malkhuta dina* ("the law of the kingdom is the law"), which was attributed to the third century CE. Babylonia sage Mar Samuel; it justified submission to Gentile rule in exchange for autonomy over communal religious affairs. This principle became the foundation of a strategy of accommodation—we might even call it a political theory—that undergirded Jewish life in the diaspora.

This principle was operative not just in Ashkenazic lands, but also in the Jewish communities that came under the rule of the new Muslim faithful as of the seventh century. It was there, under the Islamic crescent, that the largest number of Jews would dwell in the Middle Ages. The scope of Muslim control quickly extended well beyond the Middle East into Europe, initially reaching Spain in 711 CE, where a vibrant interreligious culture took rise—and then later into the Balkans and east central Europe. As a general matter, Muslim hosts bore much less of a theological grudge than their Christian contemporaries. In fact, the status of Jews as "people of the book," meant that they merited protection, although they were to be clearly marked as subordinate to Muslims.

Just how harshly this subordinate status was implemented varied by regime. Take, for example, the case of Maimonides, the great twelfth-century philosopher and jurist from Córdoba, Spain. His home community was overrun by the extremist Almohade invaders, who exiled him and his family to North Africa. There he lived under conditions of severe pressure; it has even been claimed that he was compelled to convert to Islam while under Almohade rule. After moving to North Africa as a teenager, he eventually made his way to Egypt, where his fortunes reversed dramatically. He became a physician to the sultan, as well as a widely respected leader in his community of Fustat, and the most celebrated scholar of his day throughout the Jewish world. To be sure, Maimonides was exceptional, with few peers as an intellectual. But his life reflects a broader trend. Although Muslim rule was not uniformly favorable toward Jews, it was under the reign of Islam that Jewish culture reached some of its grandest attainments—in philosophy, science, and poetry, as well as in the more traditional Jewish pursuit of rabbinic commentary.

Despite these successes, other Jews in the Muslim world were acutely aware of the fact that they remained in exile. Maimonides's near contemporary from Spain, Judah Ha-Levi, who lived in the late eleventh and twelfth centuries, was renowned for a series of Hebrew poems that expressed his deep yearning to leave Spain and "return" to the ancient homeland. One of the most poignant of his "Odes to Zion" opens: "My heart is in the east (land of Israel), and I am at the end of the west." While many medieval Jews may have shared this sentiment, at least as a dreamy and far-off end-of-days goal, they had neither the means nor, ultimately, the desire to make the arduous journey to the land of Israel. Ha-Levi was different. He left Spain for Palestine in the final year of his life, dying shortly after arriving from Egypt in the Promised Land. He would become a source of inspiration for Zionists nearly a millennium later, who shared his impulse to abandon what they saw as the indignities of exile.

Nation

From the first to the twentieth centuries, the typical condition of Jews was to live outside of the homeland in diaspora communities of diverse sizes and locations around the world. But how, in a world before instantaneous communication, did Jews in these communities manage to be in touch with one another? What, if anything, held them together? It would be far too simple to say that Jews had a coherent and fixed sense of themselves as a unified nation throughout their history.

At the same time, it is important to note that Jews internalized the idea that they had been chosen by God to become, as the Bible declared, a "great" or "holy nation"; ironically, the biblical word for "nation" is the same as the later term for a non-Jew, "goy." By the end of the Second Temple era and especially after the year 70, the distinction between Jews and Gentiles became sharp. The Jews' sense of difference from Gentiles was animated by the belief that they had a unique relationship to God, as well as a strong shared fate with their co-religionists. The canonical text of rabbinic Judaism, the Talmud, institutionalized this principle by declaring that "all Israel are responsible for one another."

This sense of collective responsibility existed within individual communities of Jews, particularly when they faced hostility or violence from their non-Jewish hosts. But it also had a life beyond the local community in the feeling of empathy and concern that Jews had for the well-being of other Jews near and far. Prior to modern times, it was common for Jews from a given community to welcome Jewish visitors for the Sabbath, providing them with lodging, kosher food, and a prayer quorum.

That said, due to limitations of both transportation and communication, it was uncommon for Jews to have frequent contact with other Jews from distant sites until the twentieth century. In lieu of direct physical contact, there was a vibrant epistolary world in medieval times in which Jews corresponded with other Jews about business or other matters, frequently using Hebrew, which was their written, though not spoken, common language. Within that world of letters, both individuals and communities often turned to rabbinic luminaries beyond their region for elucidation of questions of Jewish law. For example, the Geonim, leaders of the prestigious Talmudic academies in Babylonia from the seventh to the eleventh centuries CE, received written queries from Jews in neighboring countries and answered in the form of *responsa* that re-posed the questions and provided detailed answers. In this way, the Geonim reached beyond Babylonia to create a wider transnational community united by a shared commitment to Jewish law and values. Reflecting his status as the most prominent Jewish figure of his day, Maimonides played a similar role, entertaining questions from around the Middle East and Europe through which he provided guidance on important legal issues. He also provided emotional support to communities in times of distress, as he did in his *Epistle to Yemen* (1172) in which he expressed deep concern over the threat of forced apostasy in that country. Abandoning his usual reserve, Maimonides consoled the Jews of Yemen by suggesting that this threat was an indication of imminent messianic redemption.

Concern for fellow Jews in need was a pillar of the collective identity of Jews throughout much of their history, along with a steadfast commitment to *halakhic* observance, belief in their unique relationship with God, and hope for messianic redemption in the land of Israel. With the advent of the modern period, Jews demonstrated a new capacity to interact with and offer assistance to fellow Jews beyond their own communities. For example, in 1744, European Jews worked to overcome the expulsion order of Jews from Prague issued by Habsburg empress Maria Theresa. In 1840, European and American Jews led by Englishman Moses Montefiore intervened to prevent further assaults against Jews falsely accused of ritual murder in Damascus. This latter episode paved the way for the creation in 1860 of the Paris-based Alliance

Israélite Universelle (AIU), one of the most important
international Jewish aid organizations to emerge in this period.

The Hebrew name for the AIU was "Kol Yisrael Haverim"—all of
Israel are comrades; it reminds us that throughout much of their
history, Jews referred to themselves as "Israel," denoting not the
territory but a widely dispersed though singular people. It was in
the nineteenth century that Jews came to identify themselves
quite explicitly as a *nation*, akin to the many groups in Europe
who asserted their own distinct historical paths and claims to
national sovereignty at that time. An early proponent was the
nineteenth-century Galician thinker Nachman Krochmal, who
emphasized that the Jewish nation was pulled above the normal
cycles of history by a "new and revitalizing spirit."

By the end of the nineteenth century, references to the Jews as a
nation were common, and Jewish nationalism had developed
many ideological variants. A major line of distinction was between
the Zionists, for whom the Jewish nation must realize its right to
dwell in its homeland (the land of Israel, or Palestine), and the
Diasporists, for whom the Jewish nation must receive the right
to cultural autonomy in the diaspora. Each group had its own
political objectives: whereas Zionist Theodor Herzl expounded
the ideal of a Jewish nation-state, the Autonomist Simon Dubnow
agitated for the protection of the Jewish nation under the
framework of a sovereign state. The common denominator to
both camps was the belief that Jews had a unique national culture
and history of which to be proud. Indeed, Jewish nationalists,
and particularly Zionists, sought to instill a strong sense of group
honor in the face of the menacing modern forces of antisemitism
and assimilation. In response, Zionists grew increasingly
committed in the 1930s to their plan to establish a Jewish state
in Palestine as a haven of refuge.

In this same period, ill-disposed Gentiles began to amplify the
claim they had been making for decades that Jews were an alien

group incapable of maintaining loyalty to their host countries. They included Adolf Hitler, the decommissioned Austrian-born German soldier who began to propagate his toxic Nazi ideology focused on the desire to rid the world of Jews.

Race

At the heart of Hitler's anti-Jewish ideology was the criterion of race. In his worldview, Germans belonged to the superior Aryans whose purity was endangered by the Jews, a subhuman race. Nazis did not make distinctions: Jews of every imaginable place of origin, religious affiliation, and political ideology were cast as inescapably inferior.

This racial project drew upon decades of demeaning imagery and quasi-scientific claims associated with the modern phenomenon of antisemitism. Although hatred of Jews had existed in many forms prior to the modern age, the term *antisemitism* was coined by journalist Wilhelm Marr in the 1870s in Germany, a milieu marked by serious economic, social, and political instability. The new self-designated antisemites saw the Jews as a lurking danger, but not because of their religious beliefs nor their peculiar dress, linguistic, or dietary practices. On the contrary, Jews had assimilated into Germany society, shedding visible signs of difference and even choosing to convert to Christianity in sizeable numbers. At that point, they could enter undetected into any corner of German national life, contaminating all that they touched with their racial inferiority.

Previous forms of anti-Jewish expression focused on the radical external differences of the Jew. From the twelfth century, Christian culture in Europe developed a large corpus of visual images of Jews, often attributing to them negative physical characteristics (devil-like, foul-smelling, unhygienic, possessing horns and tails, menstruating males) that issued from their status as alleged killers of Jesus Christ.

Somewhat later, in early modern Spain, former Jews who had converted to Christianity in the waves of mass conversion over the course of the late fourteenth and fifteenth centuries faced "purity of blood" statutes introduced in the city of Toledo in 1449. The intent of these statutes was to separate "Old Christians" from "New Christians" (i.e., converted Jews), who were rendered ineligible for public office.

This impulse to distinguish people based on blood anticipated a key tenet of modern racialist discourse. Blood came to be seen as a determinant of racial purity in nineteenth-century debates about the evolution of humans. Alongside Charles Darwin's iconic *On the Origin of Species* (1859), this debate included those who were intent on establishing fixed racial hierarchies, such as the German composer Richard Wagner in *Judaism in Music* (1850) and the French diplomat Arthur de Gobineau in *Essay on the Inequality of the Human Races* (1853–1855).

While Jews were often targeted in this new discourse, they also acquired fluency in the idiom of racialism, which was an ironic reflection of the extent of their integration into European society. Jewish scholars in the early twentieth century, such as Elias Auerbach, Maurice Fishberg, Arthur Ruppin, and Ignaz Zollschan, engaged in the study of anthropology, statistics, physiognomy, and phrenology (measurements of the skull) much as their non-Jewish contemporaries did. They had twin goals: to bring glory to the Jewish race and to elevate the study of race to the rank of a legitimate scientific discipline.

Beyond these narrow circles, Jews in Europe and North America frequently invoked the language of race and blood when describing themselves. Their invocation, even though intended to honor Jews, strikes an unsettling note. After all, it was race—and more particularly, the assertion that Jews were an inferior race—that drove the Nazi campaign to annihilate them. Hitler formalized the racial distinctions between Aryans and Jews at a

Nazi Party meeting in Nuremberg in 1935, which produced
a highly detailed scheme of racial classification that became
a platform for mass murder.

In light of this history, one approaches claims of racial or
biological characteristics of a given group with trepidation. And
yet, the dramatic advances in understanding the human genome
over the past half century have prompted scientists, often Jewish
themselves, to aver that Jews possess deeply rooted genetic
affinities that distinguish them from other groups. These unique
properties lead, they claim, to a Jewish proclivity not only toward
certain kinds of mental and physical ailments, but also toward a
higher-than-average IQ. One of the most prominent researchers
of Jewish genetics today, Harry Ostrer, builds on the work of the
early-twentieth-century Jewish racial scientists in his book
Legacy: A Genetic History of the Jewish People, especially in
concluding that the "evidence for biological Jewishness has
become incontrovertible." Expanding on this claim, some scholars
have argued that Jewish genes can be found among various
unlikely groups around the globe, including the Lemba tribe in
southern Africa. Not surprisingly, the work of Ostrer and
like-minded colleagues has generated stiff criticism that disputes
the notion of a shared Jewish genetic origin.

Most Jews in the world, mindful of the Holocaust, would probably
eschew use of race or biology in defining themselves. They *would*
likely acknowledge an enduring, though often unarticulated, sense
of connection to fellow Jews, triggered by past memories,
particularly of trying events. They might even speak colloquially
and unscientifically of a Jewish "gene," for example, when
expressing a measure of pride at the high percentage of Jewish
Nobel laureates.

That said, variations abound among Jews in defining themselves.
Jews in Israel, the largest body in the world, tend to identify
themselves with the state of which they are citizens. Jews in the

United States, the second largest group in the world, tend to identify on a different basis. Whereas earlier generations saw themselves as Jews by religion, a study by the Pew Research Center in 2013 reveals that more than 60 percent of American Jews today identify principally with their shared "ancestry or culture."

These most recent attempts at self-identification recall for us two related points. First, Jewish identity, like Jewish history itself, has never been a static proposition; from their humble desert origins, Jews have continually reimagined and renamed themselves—and been renamed by others—in response to shifting historical circumstances. And second, despite the constant change in their modes and names of self-identification, Jews have managed to hold on to a shared sense of history and fate that finds few parallels in history.

Chapter 2
Numbers

If measured in chronological terms, Jews are the Methuselah of peoples, like the biblical figure who was said to have lived to the age of 969. If measured in demographic terms, however, they are a minuscule group that barely registers. As of 2015, it was estimated that there were some 14 million Jews, amounting to .2 percent of the world's population. Although Jews have been around for thousands of years, they have the same number of members as the Church of Jesus Christ of Latter-day Saints (Mormons), which was founded in the nineteenth century. Their survival may well be impressive, but the fact that they have so few members calls out for explanation. Why didn't they accumulate a much larger population?

The twin factors that help explain the Jews' survival—antisemitism and assimilation—have also served as constraints on their growth. Over the course of millennia, Jews married into, converted to, and joined other groups, sometimes through coercion and sometimes not, to the point of disappearance. At the same time, they have been subjected to persecution, expulsion, and violence, at times murderous, that diminished their numbers. Indeed, shortly after reaching their greatest demographic heights, in 1939, their numbers were tragically reduced by the genocidal Nazi assault from approximately 17 million to 11 million.

Today's world Jewish population overwhelmingly resides in two centers: Israel, with more than 6 million Jews, and the United States, with a figure that is usually estimated at around 5.5 million, but has been extended by some demographers to more than 9 million people. The wide disparity in calculating the American Jewish population centers on the differing ways that scholars answer the question of "who is a Jew?" For some, the traditional rabbinic criterion of matrilineal descent (that is, coming from the mother) is used, whereas for others, all those in a household with at least one self-identifying Jew are considered Jewish. Thus, the latter figure includes children of a non-Jewish mother and a Jewish father. An important shift in the definition of Jewish identity occurred in 1983, when the Reform branch of North American Judaism, the most ritually liberal of the three main denominations (along with Orthodox and Conservative), accepted patrilineal descent as a criterion of Jewishness. This opened up new fissures with the state-sponsored Chief Rabbinate in Israel, which held fiercely to the standard of matrilineality. It also opened up broader divisions between American Jews and the State of Israel over whether those converted to Judaism by Reform—or, for that matter, Conservative—rabbis should be considered Jews under Israel's "Law of Return," which grants an expedited path to citizenship to Jews. Within Israel itself, debates have been vigorous about the status of hundreds of thousands of new immigrants over the past three decades or so—Ethiopians and Russians who moved to Israel but were not considered Jews according to the Chief Rabbinate. These debates recall once again the dynamic nature of Jewish identity, so variable because of the constant movement of Jews from locale to locale. In the modern era, movement across national borders has become ever easier and more frequent, leading to new forms of Jewish identity, shifting centers of demographic concentration, and recurrent questions about "who is a Jew?"

How many Israelites were there?

The challenge of determining how many Jews there were in antiquity is a familiar one. For certain formative periods, the only explicit references come from the Bible. Most famously, the Book of Exodus speaks of "about six hundred thousand (Israelite) men on foot, besides women and children," who fled Egypt and wandered in the Sinai Desert. Assuming a minimal family size of four at that time, that would put the number of Israelites in the fourteenth century BCE at close to 2.5 million. Modern scholars who were experienced in historical demography cast grave doubt on such a high figure, pointing out, among other problems, that it was highly improbable that that number of people could have crossed the Red Sea in the manner described in the Bible.

The Bible actually abounds with censuses, often of soldiers. The Book of Samuel (II Samuel 24:9) identifies 1.3 million Israelite and Judean soldiers in the tenth century BCE, which would yield a Jewish population of more than 5 million (out of a world population estimated at between 50 and 100 million). This too seems far beyond the realm of the possible. A more modest estimate suggests that about 600,000 residents lived in the kingdoms of Judah and Israel in 722 BCE, in the midst of the Assyrian invasion that depopulated most of the northern kingdom and a fair bit of the southern. At the time of the Babylonian conquest of Jerusalem and the destruction of the First Temple in 586, Judah may have counted 150,000 residents. Accounts of how many residents were sent into exile in Babylonia diverge. The Book of Jeremiah (53: 28–30) writes of 4,600 men, making for an estimated total of 18,000; meanwhile, the Second Book of Kings refers to 8,000 to 10,000 men, for a total population of 40,000.

Such variations render the counting of heads in the Bible a highly imprecise proposition. Nonetheless, some number of thousands, and likely tens of thousands, of residents of Judah were settled in Babylonia in 586, where they developed new rituals that allowed them to survive the absence of the Temple. In fact, because of their rapid absorption of Babylonian culture, only a minority of the exiles opted to return to Jerusalem when afforded the opportunity by Cyrus the Great in 538 BCE.

The reconstituted Jewish community in the land of Israel grew at a relatively slow pace, at least until the Hasmonean—or Maccabean—Revolt began in 167 BCE. This rebellion of Jewish pietists against Greek rule led to the formation of a Jewish state in 140 BCE that was distinguished by its appetite for territorial expansion, pushing the country's boundaries to those in the days of Solomon's united kingdom. In the course of their expansion, the Hasmoneans encountered native populations whom they forcibly converted to Judaism, especially the southern Idumean tribe. Ironically, out of the Idumean world came the Jewish king Herod, who allied himself with the new Roman overlords of Palestine in 37 BCE and acted with brutality toward his fellow Jewish subjects.

This last stage of Second Temple history was unique in the annals of the Jews, especially the Hasmonean practice of forced conversion. Thereafter, however, the rabbis, in response to the rise of Christianity, adopted a skeptical view of conversion; they now insisted on ascertaining the sincerity of the prospects' desires to join Judaism, as well as on warning them against the risks of belonging to a small and often persecuted people. In related and characteristic fashion, they rewrote the history of the Hasmonean revolt through the holiday of Hanukah, transforming it from a glorious example of military triumph into a celebration of a religious miracle.

Jews and cities

The Hasmonean practice of conversion expanded the Jewish population of the kingdom significantly during an eighty-year reign that ended with the Roman conquest of Palestine in 63 BCE. The capital, Jerusalem, grew rapidly as the city gained new stature as a bustling urban environment.

Because of the location of the Holy Temple, Jerusalem held a special place in Jewish historical memory. But it was hardly the only urban setting in which Jews chose to live. Already in antiquity, Jews had developed a romance with cities, whose size offered them a range of religious, economic, and social opportunities that smaller rural locales did not. In the Middle Ages, Jews played an important role as agents sent by host rulers to establish new urban centers in regions that came under their control. The romance continued well into the modern age, during which Jews have exhibited a hyper-urban tendency, making their way to major cities both to escape from and to affirm their connection to fellow Jews. The proclivity of Jews for cities was grounded in a mix of factors: the presence of diverse commercial opportunities, the sense of cultural dynamism, the possibility for fleet movement, and the ability to maintain a measure of anonymity in the midst of the masses. Some of these same qualities raised the ire of antisemites in the nineteenth and twentieth centuries, who claimed that Jews were rootless urban cosmopolitans unmoored from a real connection to the land.

It was in the city that Jews achieved their greatest cultural attainments, as individuals and as a group. In 331 BCE, Alexander the Great established the Egyptian city of Alexandria, which become the world center of Hellenistic culture. It was also the site of the largest Jewish urban concentration in the world in antiquity; estimates range from 500,000 to 1 million Jewish residents in the first century CE. Alexandria was not only significant in demographic terms. It was also a site in which currents of cultural influence flowed in multiple directions. Jews were deeply drawn to Greek culture of the day, from philosophy to modes of recreation. At the same time, Greek citizens of the city were drawn to elements of Judaism, with some going so far as to observe the Sabbath and keep kosher; they were known in their day as "God-fearers." Out of this exchange emerged an amalgam of Hellenistic and Jewish cultures that left a deep imprint on members of both groups.

Meanwhile, at the behest of the Roman Empire, Jews commenced a migratory movement westward from the Middle East to Europe that continued over the first millennium of the Common Era. A particularly notable community of Jews arose in the imperial capital of Rome. The first-century Jewish historian Josephus writes of a delegation of 8,000 Roman Jews—out of a likely total Jewish population of 40,000—who received an audience with the Emperor Augustus in 4 CE.

Josephus also offered highly detailed accounts of Jewish history and demography in Palestine during the first century when Jews rose up against Roman rule and were crushed in the Great Revolt (66–70 CE). Jerusalem, as the site of the Second Holy Temple, had grown dramatically since Hasmonean times, boasting a Jewish population of perhaps a half million out of an overall population in Palestine that ranged between 1 and 2.5 million. Josephus reported that the Great Revolt generated 1.1 million fatalities (mainly Jewish), an unrealistically high figure that nonetheless captures the sense of devastation in human terms that accompanied the destruction of the Second Temple. The dénouement of the revolt against Roman rule brought to an end the period of demographic growth that began with another rebellion, the Hasmonean. Estimates suggest that the global Jewish population at this time was between 4 and 8 million (with the Roman Empire estimated at 50 million people), a range that indicates both the scale of the Jewish population and the imprecision of the methods of reconstruction.

Still, a recurrent question attends the destruction of the Holy Temple and the fall of Jerusalem. What were the immediate effects? The year 70 is often seen, and with good reasons, as an epochal turning point in Jewish history, signaling the passage from a sovereign, Temple-bound Judaism to a diasporic, rabbinic Judaism. And yet, demographic change did not occur overnight. Jerusalem invariably declined as a religious and political center. But this did not portend the end of a Jewish presence in Palestine or a massive dispersion of the Jewish population. The coastal city of Yavneh became the new center of power, where the new rabbinic leaders of post-Temple Jewish life took center stage. Scholars debate whether an exalted high court and legislative body known as the Sanhedrin also arose in Yavneh or was more of an aspirational dream of rabbis.

Just as the Temple's destruction did not end a Jewish presence in Palestine, neither did it create the Jewish diaspora. Communities had been developing outside of the land of Israel for centuries, especially in the Middle East. New communities now took rise in Asia Minor, Greece, and North Africa, as well as in Europe. To be sure, the demise of the Temple constituted an extraordinary challenge to Jews of this period, inducing mourning and a sense of entering exile once again. But Jews had already developed the capacity to adapt to new conditions in ways that permitted their survival after 70.

Jews under Islam and Christianity in the Middle Ages

There is no clear boundary separating antiquity from the medieval period of Jewish history. One noteworthy source of distinction is that the Jewish population declined precipitously from around 1 CE to 1500 CE; the decline, which may have reduced the Jewish population from 4.5 million to 1 million people, was due to a mix of factors; disease, war, mass persecution, and forced conversion.

Even with that decline, two key events in world history left a profound imprint on the evolution of Jewish history in late antiquity into the Middle Ages. First was the rise of Christianity, a direct outgrowth of the fractious world of Second Temple Judaism in the first century CE. The close family relationship between Judaism and Christianity led initially to porous boundaries between followers of the two in Palestine and neighboring countries, but later to sharply drawn lines of demarcation. Another key development in the relationship was the decision by the Roman emperor Constantine to convert to Christianity and declare it a tolerated religion in 312–313 CE. At that point, the growing theological animosity with Judaism became official imperial policy. What followed were centuries of tense relationships among Jews, Christian rulers, priests, and the general populace, with real consequences for Jewish life and demographics.

The second key event was the rise, in the first third of the seventh century CE, of Islam. Similar to the case of Constantine, the fledgling Islamic movement both married religious and political interests and sought new adherents with great zeal. As part of its extraordinarily rapid expansion, the new empire conquered Palestine and Jerusalem in the late 630s CE, building in that city two of Islam's holiest sites: the Al-Aqsa Mosque and the Dome of the Rock. From this point forward, Jews became—as they would remain throughout the Middle Ages—a small minority subject to the rule of competing monotheistic regimes, Christianity in the West and Islam in the East.

From the seventh century, the overwhelming majority of the Jewish world, some estimates are as high as 90 percent, resided in Muslim lands. An important early center of Jewish life under Islam was Spain, where Muslim rulers liberated Jews in the early eighth century from the oppressive reign of the prior Visigothic rulers and encouraged them to participate in a wide range of cultural and scientific pursuits alongside their non-Jewish contemporaries. Spain was known in Hebrew as Sepharad, a place name drawn from the biblical Book of Obadiah (1:20); Jews of Spanish origin came to be known as Sephardim, a group that served as a cultural foil to Ashkenazim in the medieval period. In the High Middle Ages, the Jews of Spain evolved into the most affluent, culturally developed, and populous community in the world, even after Christians claimed control of the Iberian Peninsula in the centuries-long *reconquista* that reached its culmination in 1492. In that fateful year, when the Spanish monarchs Ferdinand and Isabella issued their infamous Edict of Expulsion, anywhere between 80,000 to 300,000 Jews resided in the country, alongside a *converso* population likely in the tens of thousands that had converted from Judaism, often forcibly, after a wave of violence broke out in 1391.

Even as their numbers declined and they constituted a smaller percentage of the total population, Jews continued their romance with the city throughout medieval times. In both Islamic and Christian settings, cities were key centers of business and trade, and Jews played an important role in settling and developing cities from Europe to the Middle East, and even extending to China, where Jews established a large community in the Silk Route entrepôt of Kaifeng.

One especially notable urban setting was Baghdad, the city created anew in 762 CE by the Abbassid Empire, newly victorious over the Ummayads. With the Abassids intent on creating a new capital, the city developed at a blazing pace, growing into perhaps the largest city in the world with between 1 and 2 million residents by 900. Jews, for their part, had a long history in the home country, Babylonia (today's Iraq), dating back to the destruction of the First Temple. Over the course of centuries, they had developed major academies of Jewish learning, most famously, in Sura and Pumbedita, presided over by the religious authorities known as Geonim. And they joined in the vibrant cultural and economic life of the new capital of Baghdad. The intrepid Jewish traveler, Benjamin of Tudela wrote in 1168 that "there were 40,000 Jews (in Baghdad) and they dwell in security, prosperity, and honor under the Caliph."

Benjamin's travelogue, the product of his decade-long journey throughout Europe and the Middle East, yielded detailed accounts not only of Baghdad, but also of Jewish urban centers in Spain, France, Italy, Greece, Turkey, Palestine, Egypt, and Babylonia.

Jews were found in other parts of the world where Benjamin may not have gone, though about which he wrote: India and China as well as Persia, Yemen, the Arabian Peninsula, and North Africa.

Benjamin concluded his travelogue with an idealized portrait of Jews in northern France and Rhineland Germany that may or may not have reflected an actual encounter. In any event, it was in this part of Europe that, according to most scholars, Ashkenazic Jewry originated. It is somewhat mysterious why the term "Ashkenaz," which is found in a number of places in the Bible (Genesis 10: 3, 1 Chronicles 1: 6), came to refer to this region. So too is the precise path of Jews to this region of Europe. In all likelihood, the forebears of medieval Ashkenazim began their path in the ancient Middle East, most likely Palestine (but perhaps also Babylonia), journeying over the course of a millennium through North Africa and Italy before ascending to Germany.

A number of recent scholarly theories about the origins of Ashkenazi Jewry challenge or complicate this account. One of them argues controversially that eastern European Askhkenazic Jews did not have their origins in the Rhineland region, but rather emanated from the Khazars, a Turkic people from the northern Caucasus area. This iconoclastic view has not gained widespread support among scholars. But the traditional understanding of Ashkenazi origins *has* been altered by recent genetic research, whose main aim is to identify diseases common to Ashkenazi Jews. On the basis of their analysis, genetic researchers have formulated the rather startling thesis that while Ashkenazic males likely derived from the Middle East, Ashkenazi women came from Europe. This suggests that Jewish men migrated to Europe, where they married local women who were not born Jewish but converted and became absorbed into Judaism over time. It was the resulting unions, one may surmise, that created small communities of Jews who lived in close proximity to Christian neighbors throughout the Rhineland region. Often they lived in relative stability with the non-Jewish population, coming to know the language of the land and sharing with Christians a knowledge of each other's customs. These communities encouraged a robust commercial life in which Jews traded with fellow Jews and non-Jews alike; they also placed a great deal of emphasis on supporting outstanding religious institutions and scholars in their midst.

The high reputation of Ashkenazic rabbinic culture stood in telling contrast to the low population numbers of the community. Some estimate that at the beginning of the fourteenth century, 450,000 Jews lived in western, central, and eastern Europe out of a total European population of 44 million. A more recent estimate is dramatically lower, suggesting a northern European Jewish population of 25,000. Notwithstanding this sharp divergence, there is no doubt that Jews experienced a significant decline in population in the passage from the ancient to medieval periods.

The relative stability of daily life for Jews in Ashkenaz was undone on three notable occasions in the Middle Ages. First, in the year 1096, European Christians heeded the call of Pope Urban II to liberate Palestine from the hands of the Muslim infidels. On their way to the Holy Land, the Crusaders encountered Rhineland Jewish communities and, *without* Church warrant, set about to destroy those whom they held responsible for the crime of deicide (the murder of Jesus). A number of Jewish communities (Speyer, Worms, and Mainz) were destroyed, and perhaps as many as thousands of Jews lost their lives. And yet owing to their resilience and the support of local officials, Jews were able to reconstitute their communities relatively quickly.

Second, in 1290, the first act of mass expulsion against the Jews of medieval Europe was executed by King Edward I of England, to be followed by expulsions from France in the fourteenth century and culminating in the sweeping expulsion of the Jews from Spain in 1492. This attempt to rid European countries of their Jews took place against a backdrop of intensified anti-Jewish expression and imagery in popular Christianity, even though the wave of expulsions did not succeed in putting an end to Jewish life in Europe.

Related to the trend of expulsion was a third event, the "Black Plague" of the 1340s, the devastating contagion that killed tens of millions of people, diminishing Europe's population by as much as 50 percent. Jews were not only among the victims of the plague. They were also falsely accused of spreading the plague by various means, including by poisoning wells.

To be sure, not all Christians desired to remove Jews from their midst. And yet, these three developments took their toll on European Jews, forcing them to hone their ability to rebound from crisis. At times, they returned to their erstwhile homes; at other times, they moved from danger zones to safer environs. In the wake of the Black Death, Ashkenazic Jews pushed eastward into Poland, Lithuania, and Ukraine. It is this large region that would become the heartland of a pious, Yiddish-speaking population, growing from thousands of Jews in the fourteenth century to more than 6 million in 1900 and making it by that point the largest Jewish community in the world several times over. This trajectory is the reverse of the path followed by Jews under Islam, who were a vast majority of the total Jewish population in the Middle Ages but a small minority by the twentieth century.

The Spanish Expulsion and its ripples

One of the great disruptions experienced by Jews prior to the modern age occurred in Spain with the Edict of Expulsion in 1492. Since the capture of Spain by the Umayyad regime in 711, Christians sought to regain control over the Iberian Peninsula in a sustained effort called the *reconquista* (reconquest). The culmination of this effort came nearly eight centuries later in 1492, when the last Muslim forces were vanquished at Granada and the Jews were forced to leave. The edict of expulsion tore asunder the established Spanish-Jewish community, severing the groups of *conversos* from the unconverted Jews with whom they had been living in a tense equilibrium for a hundred years.

A substantial number of Jews opted not to leave their native country and chose to convert to Catholicism. For those who did choose to leave, it was an act akin to the destruction of the Second Temple, as if they had entered a second exile. And yet, the sense of despair did not prevent a large number of Jews from taking leave and creating a new Sephardic diaspora. Initially, the largest group of exiles, perhaps 25,000, made their way to neighboring Portugal, where they stayed until the Portuguese king, son-in-law of Ferdinand and Isabella of Spain, converted the Jews in 1497. Propelled to search for pockets of religious freedom, the Spanish exiles made their way to various corners of the Muslim Ottoman Empire, including Constantinople, Salonika, and Sarajevo. By the mid-sixteenth century, Constantinople had 50,000 Jews, a mix of Spanish exiles, native Jews known as Romaniot, Italians, and Ashkenazim who were organized into scores of religious communities according to their cities of origin. Spanish exiles also made their way to the northern Palestinian city of Safed, which they transformed into the most populous city in Palestine (with some 7,000 Jews). It was in Safed that they played a leading role in developing a powerful new form of Jewish mysticism known as Lurianic Kabbalah, which was then exported westward to Europe by emissaries.

If Ottoman lands became the center of a new eastern Sephardi diaspora, Christian Europe became the home of a western dispersion. Spanish exiles, as well as *conversos* who wanted to end the duplicity of their existence as outward Christians, made their way in the fifteenth century to Italy, France, England, Germany, and the Low Countries. Insofar as some of these countries had previously expelled their Jews, the new arrivals set about gingerly, revealing very gradually their Jewish origins and customs in cities from Venice to London. Some of these settings proved more tolerant than others, especially those that had fallen under the arc of the sixteenth-century Protestant Reformation, whose guiding motto of *Sola Scriptura* indicated a renewed appreciation for the Bible, the Hebrew language, and, in some cases, Jews themselves.

One such Protestant setting was the Dutch capital of Amsterdam. It was there that Spanish exiles made their way in the sixteenth century, creating a rich cultural and commercial center. In fact, it was from Amsterdam that Jewish representatives of the Dutch West Indies Company ventured forth to the Americas, landing in Recife, Brazil, in the 1630s and creating there a community of several thousand souls. Sephardic Jews of Dutch origin would go on to establish communities over the course of the seventeenth century in Dutch Guiana (present-day Suriname) and Curaçao, as well as in Charleston, South Carolina, New Amsterdam (New York), and Newport, Rhode Island.

The long reach of the Sephardi diaspora enabled wide-ranging trade in goods, ideas, and even religious aberrations. In the last third of the seventeenth century, a young Jew born in the eastern Sephardi city of Izmir, Turkey, galvanized the Jewish world with claims that he was the messiah. Hundreds of thousands of Jews joined together in the fervent hope that this messianic figure, Shabtai Zevi, would transport them from their homes in exile to the homeland in the Land of Israel. When the Ottoman Sultan arrested him in 1666 and gave him the choice between conversion and death, Shabtai Zevi converted to Islam. For a small number of his followers, his conversion did not mean the end of the messianic dream; rather, it required following the leader into Islam, where they developed a curious amalgam of Muslim and Jewish practices. (Traces of this group, the Dönmeh, can be found

even today in the Republic of Turkey.) For the majority of
Shabtai Zevi's excited followers, his conversion to Islam meant
the crushing end of their hopes of overcoming the indignity
of exile.

Some scholars have suggested a link between the anti-
establishment nature of Shabtai Zevi's movement and the
displacement and murder of tens of thousands of eastern
European Jews in Ukraine less than twenty years earlier, during
the Chmielnicki massacres (1648–1649). Jews had been sent by
Polish Catholic authorities to settle and establish commercial
outposts in Ukraine. They were received with hostility by local
Ukrainian Orthodox tribesmen, who resented both their presence
as Jews and the intrusion of Catholic Poland onto their lands. The
Cossack leader, Bogdan Chmielnicki, led an uprising directed
against Poland that unleashed massive violence against nearby
Jews, as powerfully described by a contemporaneous Jew, Nathan
Hanover, in *Yeven metsulah* (Abyss of despair). Estimates are that
between 20,000 to 100,000 Jews were murdered, a stunning loss
that concluded the centuries-long period of growth and tranquility
for Jews in eastern Europe.

While the connection between the Chmielnicki massacres and
Shabtai Zevi cannot be proved, it is clear that these two events not
only left behind tattered hopes for redemption, but also paved the
way for novel forms of spiritual and cultural expression that defied
the old order of the rabbis. Chief among these new forms was the
popular pietist movement known as Hasidism that surfaced in the
eighteenth century and drew hundreds of thousands of adherents
in the nineteenth. Rooted in the principles of Lurianic Kabbalah
and opposed to the elitism of the traditional rabbinic culture of
eastern Europe, Hasidism had a powerful vitalizing impact that
continues to this day.

By the time of Hasidism's first appearance, even with the losses
from the Chmielnicki massacres, the pendulum of demographic

balance had swung from the Islamic East to Christian eastern Europe. In 1700, the largest number of Jews in the world, more than a half million out of 1.1 million, lived in eastern Europe. From this point forward, the Jewish population in eastern Europe would grow exponentially over the next two and a third centuries until the Holocaust.

The modern age: growth and loss

From the time of the Enlightenment, the standard way of dividing Jewish—and other—history was according to the conventional three-part scheme of ancient, medieval, and modern periods. More recently, scholars have excavated an "early modern" period of history, roughly between the sixteenth and eighteenth centuries, in which a number of the most characteristic features of modernity already appear in play. Among the qualities that define the age are accelerated mobility, a heightened sense of communal cohesiveness, an explosion of new forms of knowledge, a crisis of rabbinic authority, and the blurring of religious identities. To these we may add two important demographic trends: the reversal of the precipitous population declines of the Middle Ages and the emergence of Europe as the demographic center of the Jewish world.

All of these currents continued to flow into the modern age, especially demographic growth. The world Jewish population more than doubled from 1700 to 1800, reaching 2.7 million. The next one hundred years witnessed a more than threefold increase, as the world Jewish population reached 8.7 million in 1900—and then doubled again by 1939.

What can explain this staggering growth? Dramatically improved health patterns and behavior in the modern age contributed a great deal. It is important to note that Jews had a long association with health and hygiene prior to this era. Jews were overly represented in the medical profession already in the Middle Ages;

they were often favored as court physicians, and they had access to university medical schools well before they were permitted entry to other faculties. This strong association carried forward to the modern age as well, as reflected in the disproportionate numbers of Jewish medical students in European universities. In the mid-1880s, Jewish students constituted more than 40 percent of the population at the University of Vienna Medical School, though only 10 percent of the city's population; in Berlin, they were nearly 35 percent of the medical students, but 5 percent of the overall population.

Of course, the mere presence of Jewish doctors cannot explain Jewish population growth in the modern era. First and most significantly, Jews were part of a massive demographic expansion globally, with the world population rising from an estimated 800 million in 1800 to 1.5 billion in 1900—and Europe's from 150 to 290 million during the same period. Second, Jews exhibited better rates of key health indicators than the general public: smaller, but healthier families; lower rates of disease, infant mortality, and overall death; and higher rates of breast-feeding mothers, among others. Third, even more than before, Jews became urban dwellers par excellence, one consequence of which was that they had better access to high-quality health care than rural dwellers. The modern city was also a setting in which Jews could build on their considerable economic experience with fewer formal restrictions and thereby achieve a high degree of economic stability. As a result, by the early twentieth century, large Jewish concentrations could be found in cities across the globe, including Baghdad (one-third of the population), Salonika (50 percent), Warsaw, Łódź, Budapest, Vienna, Berlin, Paris, London, New York, and Buenos Aires. Indeed, 25 percent of the world's Jewish population lived in a mere fourteen cities in 1925.

The concurrent rise in markers of good health and population numbers suggests to us that the modern period of Jewish history was wholly good for the Jews. A common starting point for this era is the eighteenth-century Enlightenment movement, which elevated the criterion of human reason to a position of preeminence. According to key Enlightenment thinkers, if all human beings were endowed with the capacity for reason, then the same logic must apply to Jews.

In some cases, this principle was implemented in ways that opened new doors for Jews. The Enlightenment gave birth to political emancipation, which granted new rights of citizenship to Jews, albeit in fits and starts. It also paved pathways for Jews to engage with non-Jewish neighbors and colleagues as well as to craft new forms of cultural and religious expression compatible with the enlightened spirit of the time. But in other cases, the Enlightenment encouraged and even pressured Jews to take the ultimate rational step and remove lingering vestiges of Jewishness through intermarriage and conversion. In the very urban settings in which Jews were so prominently represented, rates of intermarriage rose throughout the nineteenth and early twentieth centuries, reaching 30 percent or more in Berlin, Hamburg, Copenhagen, and Trieste. By comparison, in the United States, which has been as hospitable a setting for Jews as any in their history, intermarriage rates among Jews were very low throughout the twentieth century—7 percent in 1957—but have since grown many times over, reaching 58 percent in 2013.

In similar fashion, the pace of conversion from Judaism to Christianity picked up in Europe during the nineteenth century. The German poet Heinrich Heine, himself a Jew who converted to Christianity, declared that baptism was the Jew's "ticket of admission" to European society. More than 200,000 Jews followed Heine's path, principally in central and western Europe, over the course of the nineteenth century; they were a small, but clearly identifiable, stream within the overall Jewish population. In many instances, the primary impetus for conversion was not the allure of the Christian faith, but the fact that conversion could help overcome the formal and informal obstacles blocking Jews' path toward full integration into Gentile society. Indeed, during the nineteenth century, Jews often had to convert to assume university professorships and civil service jobs in European countries.

A different kind of uprooting took place in eastern Europe, where enlightenment and emancipation advanced more slowly. There, in the sprawling Russian Empire, the significant movement at hand was not from one religion to another, but rather physical movement in the form of mass exodus. The conventionally assumed trigger point was the assassination of Tsar Alexander II in 1881, in the wake of which a wave of violent pogroms directed against Jews broke out in Russia. It was at this time that the first of the huge waves of Jewish emigration from eastern Europe occurred, laying the ground for yet another rebalancing of the global Jewish population. It is estimated that almost 4 million Jews left Russia, Austria-Hungary, and Romania between 1880 and 1929, nearly two-thirds of whom came to the United States, which was now transformed into a major Jewish demographic center. Other notable areas of resettlement included Great Britain, Canada, Argentina, South Africa, Australia, and pre-state Palestine.

In the 1930s, when antisemitism became state policy in Germany, the millions of Jews who remained in eastern and east central Europe sought to escape the noose of Nazism. Hitler's expansion of the German Reich through annexation and war brought more and more of them under his control. Tragically, the gates of safe passage had largely been shut by the 1930s, both by Hitler's forces and by prospective hosts fatigued by the previous decades of immigration to their countries (e.g., the United States) or fearful of upsetting the political balance (e.g., the British in Palestine). Trapped on the European continent, more than 8 million European Jews faced the direct fury of the Nazi genocidal regime. Initially placed in centralized ghettos and camps that pockmarked the map of Europe, they began to be murdered on a mass scale commencing with Operation Barbarossa in the Soviet Union in the summer of 1941. In January 1942, German government and Nazi party officials gathered at the Wannsee Conference to decide on a master plan for a "final solution" to the Jewish Question. From that point, the pace of the extermination campaign accelerated. By the end of World War II in 1945, with Europe in smoldering disarray, the balance sheet of Nazism's destruction defied imagination: between 5.2 and 6 million Jews, representing a third or so of the world Jewish population, had been murdered.

Among the millions of refugees roaming homeless in postwar Europe were Jewish survivors of the Holocaust, 250,000 of whom made their way to "displaced persons" camps in Allied-controlled Germany, Austria, and Italy. In the coming years, several hundred thousand of them emigrated, often illegally, to Palestine—or, after 1948, to the State of Israel, which welcomed them. (In 2015, there were an estimated 189,000 Holocaust survivors living in Israel.)

Meanwhile, the new State of Israel, whose population at its inception in 1948 was just over 800,000, absorbed more than a quarter million Jewish immigrants from Arab lands in its first four years—and hundreds of thousands more in the later 1950s. These Jews, whose ancestors had often lived peaceably with their neighbors in Middle Eastern countries in the past, faced increasing hostility during the 1940s from both government authorities and the populace. In one notorious episode known as the "farhud," a pogrom fueled by pro-Nazi rhetoric was unleashed against the Jews of Baghdad in June 1941, resulting in nearly 200 Jewish deaths and large-scale property destruction. Four years later, the newly established Arab League responded to the growing strength of the Zionist movement by calling for a boycott of Jewish goods and services produced in Palestine.

After the founding of Israel in 1948, Jews from Middle Eastern countries faced additional discrimination, threats, and expropriation. Many of them made their way to the new state, joining hundreds of thousands of survivors from Europe. The presence of Jews from around the world has been a source of remarkable human vitality for the Jewish state. But it has also been an obstacle to a cohesive society. Since its establishment, Israel has continually encouraged waves of immigrants to "make *aliyah*" (that is, immigrate), including most recently Ethiopians and Russians, who have been integrated to varying degrees of success. In the complex social mix of Israel today, a more pressing demographic and political challenge exists: how to make fuller stakeholders of two key groups in society—the Palestinian Arab population, which represents 20 percent of the population at present, and the *haredim*, or ultra-Orthodox, who constitute about 10 percent. Neither group sees itself as part of the Israeli Jewish mainstream, although both will likely carve out an ever-larger share of the Israeli population in the next half century. That next phase of history will be decisive in shaping the face of Israel as it addresses its own demographic diversity in the midst of a hostile and troubled region.

With Israel as one axis, the United States is the other major demographic center of world Jewry. The two countries have, according to most analysts, comparable numbers of Jews—between 5 to 6 million each. Akin to Israel, the United States evinces both positive and less positive sociological signs. On the one hand, Jews are among the most educated and affluent members of American society, and they have achieved a degree of economic and political security that is without precedent in Jewish history. On the other hand, their successful integration in the United States has led to unmistakable signs of disaffiliation and alienation, one of which is the high intermarriage rate. American Jewish leaders from an older generation express anxiety over retaining younger members who do not share their vision of a holistic community, but rather relate to their Jewishness in a more individualized and often "virtual" way, aided by new forms of social media.

This reliance on social media marks yet another kind of movement, a twenty-first-century successor to the waves of migration that have continually reoriented Jewish communal life over the ages. Jews have proved exceptionally adept at moving, a fact of life necessary both to explore new opportunity and to evade persecution. They have also demonstrated a strong ability to adapt to the new circumstances in which they find themselves.

All of these accrued skills of adaptation have been called into play in the modern age, which has posed new and daily challenges to Jews. In demographic terms alone, tremendous population growth has been followed by massive decline, which has then been followed again by replenishment. What the future holds remains an open question. The coming decades will witness a contest between demographic growth, especially in Israel, and decline, largely in the diaspora. That said, it is reasonable to assume that over the next quarter century, the Jewish people will equal or surpass the peak set before World War II of 17 million souls.

Chapter 3
Cultures

In making their way through history, Jews frequently lived out a form of God's self-description in the Book of Zechariah (4:6). "'Not by might nor by power, but by my Spirit,' says the Lord Almighty." For only a small portion of their history did they possess an army of their own to defend themselves; neither military force nor political power, in the form of a state, was a prominent feature of their existence or a key to their survival.

The traditional Jewish explanation was that God's "spirit" protected the people Israel as part of an inviolable covenant between them. But it was a more mundane factor that allowed Jews to survive as a small and often powerless minority. And herein lies one of the most curious and ironic features of Jewish history. Even in the face of Gentile hostility, Jews engaged in a constant process of cultural interaction with the societies in which they lived. They drew from and reshaped the habits and values of the surrounding world. And they did so by balancing this engagement with preservation of the distinctive traditions of their group.

The result of this balancing effort was an evolving series of Jewish cultures (plural) rather than a single unified culture. Together these cultures constitute a richly marbled admixture of local customs and shared global practices. It is important to emphasize that this mosaic was not a product of the modern era alone, which one might assume given the rapid pace of Jewish assimilation from the nineteenth century on. On the contrary, "assimilation" has been a constant feature of Jewish life insofar as Jews have continually adapted to new circumstances and environments they encountered in their dispersion. Rather than resist the cultural markers of these new settings, as their religious leaders implored them to do, Jews repeatedly absorbed the languages, names, dress, and social customs of their host societies. This work of absorption operated at all levels of cultural production, from rarefied philosophical and legal scholarship to daily habits found in the home. The large body of Jewish customs known as *minhagim* drew from surrounding cultures, whether it be the medieval Ashkenazi practice of interrupting public prayer to air a grievance or the Middle Eastern practice of striking your neighbor with scallions at the Passover table while singing the song "Dayenu."

Given their rootedness in the daily practices of the home, women played an especially significant role in transmitting *minhagim*. One notable and poignant site of transmission was the Iberian Peninsula during the time of the Inquisition. A minority of Jews who had become Catholics in the waves of forced conversion that began in 1391 chose to preserve what vestiges of Jewish ritual that they could in secret. The burden of responsibility for these "crypto-Jews" fell on women, who cultivated Jewish practices in the only safe space they had, the privacy of the home.

In general, *minhagim*, which varied widely by locale, lent diversity and vibrancy to Jewish culture. At times, the cultural differences produced pitched rivalries among communities. The prototypical cultural competition, based on differing scholarly and cultural traditions, was between Babylonia and Palestine in the first centuries of the Common Era. The two communities had distinct political, legal, and scholarly authorities, and each produced its

46

own monumental bodies of rabbinic literature, culminating in the Babylonian and Palestinian Talmuds. So prominent and self-assured was the Babylonian community toward its rival that one Babylonian sage is recorded as saying: "All lands are dough to Palestine, and Palestine is dough to Babylonia."

The tradition of rivalry based on differences in culture and customs continued in the medieval and modern periods, principally between Ashkenazic and Sephardic Jews. Each fostered a feeling of cultural superiority over the other, reflecting the proclivities of their native environments. For centuries, Ashkenazic Jews believed that they were more stringent and pious in observance than Sephardim, who deemed themselves more culturally enlightened and sophisticated. Disdain toward the other could reach such a point that the Dutch Sephardic philosopher Isaac de Pinto cautioned in 1762 that "if a Portuguese Jew in England or Holland married a German Jewess, he would of course lose all his prerogatives, be no longer reckoned a member of their Synagogue, forfeit all civil and ecclesiastical preferments, be absolutely divorced from the body of the nation and not even be buried with his Portuguese brethren."

This sense of cultural superiority was carried forward in a number of different ways in the modern era. In the nineteenth century, German Jews looked on with a measure of admiration and longing at medieval Sephardic Jews, who represented in their eyes a successful model of cultural integration. By contrast, in the next century, the eastern European Jews in Israel, especially the political elite associated with the Labor Party, often regarded Sephardic and Mizrachi Jews as culturally inferior, and placed them upon arrival in transit camps to be reeducated for participation in the new society. The Mizrachim resented the bias they faced, leading to substantial friction in the social fabric of Israel from the 1950s onward. In the early 1970s, a group of second-generation Mizrachim, borrowing from oppositional politics in the United States, formed an Israeli Black Panther

Party. And in 1977, Mizrachim played an important role in propelling the long-time opposition Likud Party to victory over the ruling Labor Party. Since that time, social interaction between Ashkenazic and Sephardic Jews, including the once taboo practice of intermarriage, has become more common, thereby mitigating, but not eliminating, the tension.

The monotheistic revolution and ancient Jewish culture

The capacity to adapt to new cultural settings while retaining a good measure of their distinctiveness is one of the most impressive of the Jews' talents. Constantly confronted by change, they navigated the shifting currents of history with a high degree of equipoise and instinct for survival. They also managed to recalibrate their cultural identity in the wake of major outbursts of revolutionary energy, three of which have altered the complexion of Jewish history.

The first and most formative of these was the monotheistic revolution that transformed a band of desert-dwelling idol worshippers into a cohesive people with an iron-clad faith in a single God—and a religious culture molded in its image. Modern scholars have not forged a consensus on how this revolution came about. Some build on traditional accounts by pointing to a sudden theological breakthrough that led the Israelites in the time of Moses (fourteenth century BCE) to pledge allegiance to an omnipotent deity who would come to be known by the four-letter Hebrew name YHWH. Others speak of a more gradual evolution from the regnant form of polytheism in the ancient Near East to the belief in a single god, perhaps through an intermediate phase known as "monolatry" that recognized the existence of multiple gods but permitted the worship of only one.

We do not know for sure. The more gradual approach would seem to dilute the drama and force of a revolution, at least in terms of origins. On the other hand, the logic of that approach lies in the recognition that Israelite monotheism, including some of its characteristic features, such as animal sacrifice, priests, agricultural festivals, and the centrality of a major flood story, emerged out of an indigenous Near Eastern culture that recognized many gods.

Yet the importance of monotheism resides less in its origins than in its effects. It not only introduced the idea of the Israelites as the "chosen people" with whom God had a unique relationship, but also brought forward a rigorous moral code rooted in the Ten Commandments that was subsequently adopted by Christianity and Islam and has become a foundation for much of Western civilization.

This new belief system was accompanied by a set of ritual practices intended to set the Israelites apart from others. In fact, these ritual practices came to be regarded over time by traditional Jews as originating at Revelation at Mt. Sinai and thereby possessing divine status. The provenance of the Oral Law, as it was known, is laid out in the opening passage from Pirke Avot, one of the tractates of the third-century Mishnah: "Moses received the Torah and handed it down to Joshua; Joshua to the Elders; the Elders to the prophets; and the prophets handed it down to the men of the Great Assembly." For rabbinic Judaism, the Oral Law was a full companion to the Written Law, each of which complemented the other to form the Dual Torah. For many modern Jews, though, including early advocates of Reform Judaism, the rituals associated with the Oral Law were man-made, not divine, having evolved over time; as a result, they lost their status as obligatory to practice.

That said, adherence to the Oral Law provided almost all premodern Jews—and continues to provide observant Jews today—with a detailed regimen to maintain their distinctive way of life. Some of the most stringently observant today hold to an ancient rabbinic legend that the survival of the Jews was predicated on their unwillingness to adopt foreign names, languages, or dress. To this day, *haredim* proudly announce their resistance to Gentile culture by forming an acronym from the Hebrew words for name (*shem*), language (*lashon*), and dress (*malbush*): *ShaLeM*, a word that connotes wholeness or completeness.

This kind of resistance seems plausible as an explanation of Jewish cultural distinctiveness except that it is altogether wrong. Jews *constantly* adopted the names, languages, and dress of their hosts. According to some scholars, they even adopted monotheism from the Egyptians in the fourteenth century BCE. Far more solid as evidence are the traces of indigenous culture—for example, the local deity Baal or the pagan prophet Balaam—that surfaced in the Hebrew Bible. The persistence of such elements in early Israelite religion was a telling indication of the open borders of early Israelite culture, but only one indication. The architecture, pottery, and tools of ancient Israelites also reveal the imprint of the surrounding society, and they point to a broader dynamic that would mark subsequent forms of Jewish culture: a conscious tendency toward marking clear boundaries *and* an unconscious process of absorbing cultural values from the host or neighboring society.

After being exiled in Babylonia in the sixth century BCE, Jews acquired the language of the empire, Aramaic, as they would in so many other new diaspora communities. And yet, the flow of cultural exchange was not one way. Just as Jews picked up new habits and norms in their transplanted home, so too they brought their own practices with them from Palestine, which they shared with their new neighbors. The marketplace, where commercial goods were hawked and social interaction proceeded, was a key site for this unspoken exchange of cultural values. It was where Jews and non-Jews met, and where the ceaseless work of mimesis—cultural imitation—proceeded.

Meanwhile, in the regions of the Middle East that, from the fourth century BCE, came under the control of the Greeks, Hellenistic culture proved to be an exceptionally powerful and irresistible allure, including and especially to Jews. It has already been noted that Philo established a reputation as a leading Jewish interpreter of Greek philosophy in Alexandria. The Jewish philosophers of Alexandria included a cohort of women associated with a band of ascetic scholars who combined intense study and trance-like meditation practices. At a less rarefied level, Jews readily adopted Greek attire, leisure, and educational practices. Alexandrian Jews of a certain status sent their children to a Jewish *gymnasium*, where they received instruction intended to nurture their bodies and minds. The absorption of Greek culture occurred without explicit declaration—and can be noticed even today. For example, when Jews recline at a Passover seder while drinking the prescribed four cups of wine, they are reenacting an ancient Greek practice.

Even the most "native" of Jewish sources, the Holy Scripture, was reframed in a Hellenistic idiom. According to the widely disseminated account in the legendary text known as the *Letter of Aristeas*, King Ptolemy invited seventy-two scholars, six from each of the twelve Israelite tribes, to draft a translation of the Pentateuch from Hebrew into Greek in the early third century BCE. The scholars spent seventy-two days on their work, the *Letter* claims, and produced a perfect translation. Building on this legend, the translated version that was included in the Library of Alexandria came to be known as the Septuagint, the translation of the "Seventy." It was deemed authoritative by many contemporary Jews, and it would serve later as the main Old Testament source for the early Christian movement.

The acquisition by Jews of Greek language and culture was restricted neither to the diaspora nor to the age of Greek hegemony over the Middle East. Even after the Roman conquest of Greece in 146 BCE, Greek continued to assert an active presence in Palestine—the very name of which appears for the first time in Greek in the fifth century. Herod, the Jewish vassal king under the Romans during the first century BCE, was a cunning and reviled ruler; however, he was also a master builder who made extensive use of Greek architectural features in the palaces, fortresses, and aqueducts that he built—and even in the reconstructed Holy Temple that was the main site of Jewish ritual devotion. Meanwhile, Josephus, the prominent Jewish general and historian of the first century CE, boasts of his ability to speak Greek, which he used to write some of his most important works. Even more surprisingly, Greek was prominently represented in the Palestinian (or Jerusalem) Talmud, offering up thousands of loan words that often provided conceptual clarity for this major foundation of rabbinic Judaism.

These examples suggest that it was not merely a matter of Jews assimilating to Greek. Greek itself became a vital ingredient in the formation—or better, *trans*formation—of Jewish culture from its early monotheistic roots. And by no means was Greek unique as a cultural tonic. From antiquity, Jews encountered languages and cultures at every turn, mobilizing them to reinforce their ever-evolving traditions. Aramaic, which had become the most popular tongue used in Palestine by the time of Jesus in the first century CE, was another example. It was the language in which the bulk of the Talmuds—the Babylonian as well as the Palestinian—was written. A quick glance at a page of Talmud reminds us that Aramaic was so deeply accepted by Jews that they rendered it sacred by writing it in Hebrew characters. Aramaic thus became an oft-replicated prototype for the adaptation of vernacular languages that yielded local Jewish tongues in Persia, the Arab-speaking world, Italy, Germany and eastern Europe, and Spain and the Sephardi diaspora, among others. This process of linguistic adaptation, it bears reiterating, constituted a fitting reflection of the way in which Jewish culture absorbed and assimilated, while still preserving its own clearly demarcated identity.

The universalizing revolution and medieval Jewish cultures

The monotheistic revolution affected every aspect of Israelite and later Jewish culture, beginning with the new theological foundation it spawned and extending to a broad range of ritual and social practices. The next revolutionary moment occurred with the rise of Christianity in the first century of the Common Era. The theological and cultural direction of Christianity moved from the particular to the universal, as articulated by Paul of Tarsus in Galatians (3:28): "There is neither Jew nor Gentile, neither slave nor free, nor is there male and female, for you are all one in Christ Jesus." According to this view, Jews were corrupted by their fastidious adherence to the letter rather than to the spirit of the Law.

Of course, one must recall that Christianity emerged in the last stages of the Second Temple period in which groups such as the Pharisees, Sadducees, and the ascetic breakaways at the desert haven of Qumran competed with one another for the mantle of Jewish authenticity. An aura of apocalyptic change hovered over the populace in first-century Palestine, as social protest, religious innovation, and political rebellion combined to form a combustible mix. Out of the ashes of the Second Temple, destroyed by Roman forces in 70 CE, a new world began to take rise. And yet, it would be a mistake to assume a total dichotomy between old and new. Not only were there currents within first-century Judaism agitating for a more inclusive outreach to Gentiles. There were also Jews drawn to Jesus and his message who were not prepared to leave behind Judaism altogether. Those so-called Jewish-Christians were an intriguing reminder that the boundaries of religious identity remained porous in this highly consequential era.

In the coming centuries, we see the emerging contours of two new entities: Christianity and its estranged sibling, rabbinic Judaism.

Born of the same parent, but separated at birth, the two regarded each other warily at first before grounding their mutual enmity in deep theological roots. Between the second and fourth centuries, Christianity becoming increasingly settled in the view that Jews were guilty of what early Church Father John Chrysostom called deicide, that is, the murder of the Christian God, Jesus Christ. This would become a theological touchstone for all subsequent Christian anti-Judaism.

Moreover, that theological principle assumed new significance in the fourth century, when Christianity became the state religion of the Roman Empire. At that point, a new era of formal restrictions on Judaism commenced. Jews, for their part, lacked sovereign political power of any sort, but they institutionalized their animosity toward Christians in religious texts and liturgy, including a prayer recited daily that inveighed against apostates and praised God for "humbling the arrogant."

And yet, Jewish-Christian relations cannot be reduced to declared theological animus. The currents of cultural exchange never stopped flowing between early Christianity and rabbinic Judaism. The two coexisted, it has been said, in "a single circulatory system" in which social and ritual practices were shared, albeit in unspoken ways. The close affinities between the holidays of Easter and Passover, both spring renewal festivals, illustrate this important process.

In more self-conscious terms, rabbinic Judaism expressly sought, after the collapse of the Great Revolt in 70, to reorganize Jewish life around the Oral Law. A story is told of Yohanan ben Zakkai, a first-century sage who was said to have predicted the ascent of the Roman general Vespasian to the position of emperor in the waning days of the revolt. In appreciation for the realization of this prediction, Vespasian granted Yohanan a wish, which the sage tersely formulated: "Give me Yavneh and her sages." He was, in essence, asking for a new site of Jewish religious culture in a world lacking the physical edifice of the Holy Temple, the service of priests, or the practice of animal sacrifice. It was in that very era that the new leaders of Judaism—who would be known as "rabbis," or teachers—sought to organize the ritual laws and practices that had circulated for centuries and present them to Jews as a program for ongoing religious commitment. The rabbis were guides in the ways of the law, as well as tireless interpreters who bore a powerful intellectual disposition to turn texts "over and over again," finding new angles and insights to understand them.

A key textual anchor for the interpretive project of the rabbis was the *Mishnah*, the first written compendium of the Oral Law that was compiled in Palestine around 200 CE. It served as the foundation for the two Talmuds; in fact, mishnaic passages anchored subsequent rabbinic discussion, and they would come to be placed at the center of the page in printed versions. Circles of scholars working in the two major intellectual centers of Palestine and Babylonia between the fourth and sixth centuries parsed these texts and then recorded their respective debates in Aramaic, placing them around the Hebrew-language *Mishnah* sources on the Talmudic page. They went about this work in a new set of institutions of learning, Talmudic academies, where they addressed a wide range of topics, from matters of ritual purity to agricultural practice to legal ethics to messianism. The most prominent academies in which this work ensued, the Babylonian centers of Sura and Pumbedita, were the Harvard and Yale of late antiquity; their leading scholars gained renown throughout the Jewish world, issuing opinions that traversed borders in what became an early transnational legal system.

From this point forward, rabbis throughout the world produced a thick body of opinions in thousands of book-length compendia. So too, they added layer upon layer of commentary on the Talmud, generating an intricate and dense system of law that covered virtually every aspect of Jewish life. Alongside Babylonia,

Ashkenaz was also an active site of this work in the Middle Ages. From the tenth century, scholars created there one of the most important centers of rabbinic legal activity. The most significant of the Ashkenazic rabbinic figures was Rashi (Rabbi Shlomo Yitshaki), who was born in Troyes, France, in the mid-eleventh century. Rashi's commentaries were so widely read and admired that when the Talmud was first printed in the late fifteenth century, they were placed on the margins of the page with the Talmudic text in in the center.

Rashi had no sons to continue in his path, but his grandsons were distinguished rabbinic scholars in their own right who attempted to complete and elaborate on their grandfather's work of commentary. The work of rabbinic commentary and legal decision making was a male preserve, which makes striking the legends that surrounded Rashi's daughters, mothers of the grandsons, to the effect that they studied and were learned in Torah. It was even said that one or more of the daughters wore *tefillin*, the black square prayer boxes placed by Jewish men (though now also some women) on the arm and head while reciting the morning prayers. Despite this legend, women did not play a leadership role in rabbinic Judaism. Indeed, it was not until the twentieth century that the Berlin-born Regina Jonas became the first woman to be ordained as a rabbi in 1935.

At one level, the dense legal world of the rabbis, both in the ancient Middle East and in medieval Europe, was an exclusive and insular fraternity. At the same time, the grand exegetical tradition of which Rashi was a master proceeded alongside and, in some sense, was in unarticulated dialogue with Christian scriptural exegesis. Rabbinic and Catholic canon law developed in similar locations and eras. And Jewish and Christian commentators alike recorded their words in lavishly adorned illuminated manuscripts that bespoke a shared material culture.

The overlap of cultures helps explain why Rashi, who wrote in a crisply lucid Hebrew style, was also a master of medieval French,

3. A Jewish teacher instructs his student, reflecting the attention placed on learning and literacy, especially for boys, in medieval Jewish life. It is drawn from the Coburg Pentateuch, a colorful fourteenth-century illuminated manuscript of the Five Books of Moses.

elements of which he incorporated into his commentaries. An even clearer sign of linguistic adoption was the emergence of Yiddish in the broader Ashkenazic culture of which Rashi was part. Most researchers maintain that Yiddish has a strong Germanic base and arose in the formative German heartland of Ashkenazic culture, perhaps by the twelfth century. Yiddish then migrated eastward to eastern Europe, which would become the largest site of Yiddish proliferation. Indeed, it is there that one could find, by the nineteenth and twentieth centuries, millions of Yiddish speakers who conducted their daily lives, wrote fine literature, and developed a robust political culture in the language. Estimates are that there were between 11 and 13 million Yiddish speakers in the world on the eve of the Holocaust. Today, Yiddish lives on as a spoken tongue almost exclusively in *haredi* or strictly Orthodox communities, where it is regarded as a vital tool of insulation against assimilation into mainstream culture.

Several centuries before Yiddish emerged as a dominant cultural force in Germanic lands, another group of Jews was adapting a major regional language to their needs in the Middle East. Similar to the rendering of Aramaic or later a version of German into Hebrew characters, Jews began to recraft Arabic into a Jewish language by writing it in Hebrew letters and importing Hebrew loan words. This effort commenced after Arabic became the language of the new Islamic empire in the seventh century.

As a general matter, Jews of Islamic lands both adopted the Arabic language and participated in the favored cultural pursuits of the host society. Most notably, Muslim scholars recovered and revived the study of philosophy from the ancient Greeks and made it a central preoccupation. Jewish scholars shared in that interest and produced the most important works of Jewish philosophy since the time of Philo. Saadya Gaon, head of a major Babylonian academy in the tenth century, was not only a master of Jewish law, but also an outstanding philosopher whose *Book of Beliefs and Opinions* (933) was the first major work in medieval Jewish philosophy. This book was surpassed in significance two centuries later when Maimonides published his monumental *Guide for the Perplexed* (*c.* 1190). Like Saadya Gaon's book, the *Guide* sought to reconcile Judaism with regnant philosophical understandings of the origins of the world, the nature of good and evil, and the quest for knowledge of God.

Significantly, these two major works were written in Judeo-Arabic. Both authors were fully at home in Arabic, as well as deeply versed in the major schools of philosophy in the Islamic world. They tailored Arabic, the language of philosophy in this period, to their specific purposes: to reach a philosophically sophisticated Jewish audience in an idiom that delineated an identifiable cultural boundary. Judeo-Arabic, written in Hebrew letters, offered an exclusive means for Jewish readers to enter into the world of Islamic philosophy.

It is significant to note the places of origin of the two major medieval Jewish philosophers to gain a sense of the geographic range of the Islamic world, as well as of the Jewish subculture within it. Saadya Gaon was born in Egypt and spent time in Palestine and Syria before being called to Babylonia to head the prestigious academy of Sura. He lived the last years of his life in Baghdad, the capital of the Abbassid Empire. In a very short period of time, the city became a major demographic and cultural center noted for its artistic, intellectual, and scientific innovation and marked by open interaction between Muslims and non-Muslims.

Maimonides, meanwhile, spent the last thirty-five years of his life in Saadya's home country of Egypt, though he was born and raised in Córdoba, Spain. From the early eighth century, Córdoba—and more generally, southern Spain, or Al-Andalus as it was known—had fallen under the control of the competing Umayyad Empire, which sought to match Baghdad as a cultural center. The Umayyad caliph Abd al-Rahman II promoted intellectual, scientific, and artistic activity among Muslims, Jews, and Christians in Córdoba. The study of philosophy flourished there, along with a diverse array of fields ranging from astronomy to poetry. Jews were active participants in this vibrant cultural world of Umayyad Spain. Figures such as Samuel ibn Nagrela, Solomon ibn Gabirol, and Abraham ibn Ezra excelled in multiple areas, combining Torah knowledge, philosophy, and poetic creativity. Their patronymics—the use of the Arabic "ibn" to connote "son of"—revealed the extent to which they and their names were part of a broader Arab-Muslim world. In fact, ibn Nagrela, otherwise known as Shmuel Ha-Nagid, was not just a member of the Andalusian cultural elite; he was also a leading Jewish courtier who ascended to the positions of general and vizier, or chief political advisor, to the king. And he was not the first Jew to attain a high position in a Muslim regime. Earlier in the tenth century, a Jewish scholar and physician named Hasdai ibn Shaprut served as chief diplomat to the caliph, while maintaining close relations with Jews throughout the world. In this sense, he was doubly loyal—to the Muslim regime he served and to his fellow Jews. Likewise, he was fully at home in both Arabic and Hebrew, with Judeo-Arabic as a key mediating tool.

Of course, a small percentage of Jews belonged to the elite intellectual and social classes. But most regarded Torah study with great reverence. Fathers instilled in their sons respect for Torah study as a key to performing religious commandments. Girls, who were not obligated to fulfill all of the religious obligations as boys, typically did not receive the same degree of Torah education as boys nor were they welcomed in schools. But they often did receive some form of informal education from their mothers.

Part of what we know about Jewish education in the medieval world emerges out of the materials collected in the Cairo Geniza. The Geniza was the repository of discarded texts kept in the Ben

Ezra synagogue in Cairo that, since its modern "discovery" by English-based researcher Solomon Schechter, has yielded an extraordinary portrait of medieval life in the Mediterranean world.

The hundreds of thousands of Geniza fragments have allowed scholars to reconstruct the far-reaching commercial ties of Jewish—and, for that matter, Muslim—merchants throughout North Africa and Europe. They also help detail the daily existence of Jews, the clothes and jewelry they wore, the design of their homes, the modes of hospitality practiced, and the food and wine they drank. The Geniza documents reveal, for example, that despite the considerable commercial acumen of Jews, perhaps a quarter of the community's population in medieval Egypt lived in poverty. The Jewish community ran an extensive network of institutions to serve the poor, animated by a deep commitment to *tsedakah*, charity, as a religious duty. Moreover, the Geniza fragments affirm how ubiquitous religion was in the lives of medieval Jews, who sought God's intercession, through prayer, in virtually all aspects of their lives, both great and small. In sum, they offer up a textured sense of Jewish life under medieval Islam.

If the great monotheistic revolution instilled in Jews an abiding belief in Divine Providence (and in their own election), it was the universalizing revolution triggered by the rise of Christianity that set in motion a new competition among monotheistic faiths in which Jews were the weakest party. But that competition did not entail the collapse and disappearance of Judaism. Rather, it impelled Jews to develop adaptive skills in order to survive, as they learned to engage in regular but selective participation in the Gentile world with a constant eye on fortifying their own religiously based culture. Simply put, medieval Jews did not live in isolation from their non-Jewish neighbors, but rather in a state of ongoing and at times tense interaction that yielded a wide variety of local cultural forms.

The secular revolution and modern Jewish cultures

By the end of the fifteenth century, a major demographic and social shift occurred in the Jewish world that had profound geographic and cultural consequences. Up to that point, the Jewish community of Spain had been the most populous, affluent, and influential in the Jewish world. During the three and a half centuries after Maimonides and his family were forced off the Iberian Peninsula in 1148, Spain was in the throes of a relentless campaign by Christians in the north of the country to capture control of southern parts from the hands of the Muslims. In the midst of this drive to create an all-Christian peninsula, Jews too came under pressure. They were subject to violent waves of forced conversions in the late fourteenth and early fifteenth centuries that generated thousands of *conversos*, some of whom maintained Jewish rituals secretly in their homes. In fact, it was in response to the "Judaizing" activity of *conversos* that the Spanish monarchs, Ferdinand and Isabella, introduced the Inquisition in Spain in 1478. Fourteen years later, they decided to complete the ethnic cleansing of Spain by expelling the Jews in 1492. Among other effects, the Edict of Expulsion marked the birth of the great Sephardic Jewish diaspora, in both its eastern (Ottoman) and its western (European) sectors.

Two towering figures of Sephardic origin, products of east and west respectively, emerged in the seventeenth century to alter the complexion of medieval Jewish culture. One was Shabtai Zevi, the Turkish-born false messiah who attracted hundreds of thousands of adherents to his movement, before he converted to Islam. The second figure came from the western Sephardi diaspora of Holland. Benedict, or Baruch, Spinoza was the descendent of Portuguese *conversos* who had moved to Amsterdam in the early seventeenth century. Like Shabtai Zevi, Spinoza grew up in a traditionally observant setting. His intellectual curiosity as a young man led him to a circle of non-Jewish free thinkers who encouraged his own unconventional thinking about Judaism, religion in general, and the relationship between church and state. Spinoza's iconoclasm led to confrontations with Jewish communal officials, culminating in his excommunication in 1656 from the Amsterdam community owing to his "horrible heresies." Spinoza never formally returned to Judaism, but neither did he convert to Christianity. Indeed, it was said of him that he was the first person to leave the confines of the Jewish community without converting.

This statement suggests that there was in Spinoza's time, and perhaps as a result of his actions, a secular revolution that carved out a space in society that was beyond the reach of religious authorities, where one could think freely and without inhibition about sensitive matters. Spinoza dwelt alone in this new "secular" space after his excommunication, during which time he wrote a number of seminal works of philosophy. In one of them, the *Theological-Political Treatise* (1670), he gave articulate voice to a host of doubts that may have prompted his exclusion from the Jewish community fourteen years earlier—about the nature of God, Israel's election, Mosaic authorship of the Bible, and the miracle of the Jewish people's survival.

The fact that he published this major philosophical work anonymously suggests that there were lingering obstacles to the free expression of radical ideas. But Spinoza did lend his powerful voice, if not always his name, to challenging ideas about God, faith, and politics. In fact, it has been argued that he stood at the center of a "radical Enlightenment" movement that preceded and was far more sweeping than the moderate Enlightenment of the eighteenth century.

If one compares Spinoza to the greatest Jewish philosopher of the eighteenth century, Moses Mendelssohn, this claim makes sense. Spinoza and Mendelssohn did share certain key beliefs—for example, in the liberating power of human reason or in a view of Judaism as rooted in laws and commandments, not eternal philosophical truths. And both men have been called the first modern, or even secular, Jew. But Spinoza went much further than Mendelssohn in challenging the social, as well as theological, foundations of Judaism. Whereas Spinoza surrendered any ongoing affiliation to the Jewish community, Mendelssohn, who was born in Dessau and moved to Berlin as a young man, remained observant throughout his life. He was frequently asked by non-Jewish colleagues why, if he were such a philosophically sophisticated man, he continued to adhere to Judaism. The question deeply frustrated him, for he believed that Judaism and the Enlightenment were thoroughly compatible.

In making this point, Mendelssohn stood at a tenuous turning point. He sought at once to affirm the continuing relevance of the Jewish religion *and* to invite his co-religionists to enter into the new cultural world of Enlightenment Germany. Toward the latter aim, he produced a Judeo-German translation of the Hebrew Bible known as the *Biur* (1780–1783) to introduce traditional Jews to the German language. He also was the founder of the distinctive Jewish variant of the Enlightenment movement called the *Haskalah*, which couched its program of educational and cultural reform in the traditional language of Hebrew.

Mendelssohn made use of both German and Hebrew, since his burden was double. He not only had to persuade fellow Jews of the benefits of Enlightenment. He also had to render Judaism understandable in the Enlightenment language of his day. He did so in his major Jewish book, *Jerusalem* (1783), in which he argued that neither Judaism nor any other religion could use coercive means to compel belief; religion was a decidedly voluntaristic matter, subject to the reason and choice of the individual.

Mendelssohn' social milieu in eighteenth-century Berlin was one in which Jews and Christians began to know one another not only from the marketplace, but also from their encounter in the city's literary salons. Many of the leading salons were run by Jewish women, who, seeking relief from the boredom of their marriages, hosted gatherings of authors, philosophers, artists, court officials, nobles, and commoners to engage in serious conversation. Here Jew met non-Jew as seeming equal, both partners in the creation of a "neutral society" in miniature that could serve as a model for a broader Enlightenment society.

And yet, the salon was, in many regards, an illusion. It catered to the upper classes who were not representative of the larger population or social dynamics in Berlin. Nor did it spell the end of anti-Jewish discrimination. Formal and informal obstacles remained in the path of Jews, preventing their entry into political office, academia, and the civil service. One prominent disciple of Mendelssohn, David Friedlander, even proposed to a Protestant cleric in 1799 that he and a group of fellow Jews convert to Christianity to gain social acceptance, but on the condition that they not be required to embrace core Christian dogmas. His offer of a "dry baptism" was rejected.

This instance makes clear that even in the seemingly secular age of the Enlightenment, religion played a key role as a marker of social identity. It also makes clear that what the Enlightenment offered was a sort of double gesture to the Jews: beckoning them to a gleaming edifice of equality while closing the door to them as they crossed its threshold. This set of conflicting signals had its distinct psychic costs. It produced a sense among Jews in the West that they were either "pariahs" or "parvenus," outcasts or upstarts, in the words of the twentieth-century thinker Hannah Arendt. Arendt herself depicted the devastating impact of this double gesture in her highly autobiographical biography of Rahel Varnhagen (née Levin). Varhnagen was born in 1771 into a wealthy Jewish family in Berlin, where she became a much sought-after literary salon host. The salon spelled, in a way, her exit from Judaism into a wider non-Jewish world. She married a non-Jew and spent much of her adult life outside of the Jewish community. And yet, she never vanquished her primal allegiances to nor, for that matter, her ambivalences about Judaism. She is said to have uttered on her deathbed: "The thing which all my life seemed to me the greatest shame, which was the misery and misfortune of my life—having been born a Jewess—this I should on no account now wish to have missed."

The perception that Jewishness was a source of shame reflected the complexity of the Jewish condition in modern Europe in the nineteenth and twentieth centuries. While Jews were perched at the border of social acceptance, they had great difficulty traversing it. The sense of being an outsider in a society with which one was now natively familiar could induce paralysis or inspire conversion, but it could also become a font of cultural innovation. Franz Kafka, the great early-twentieth-century Jewish author from Prague, captured this sense of being an outsider when he compared the Jew to a horse whose rear legs were stuck in the past and whose front legs had not yet landed in the present. Such a position permitted, even encouraged, one to break the mold of existing convention, as Kafka did by upending the linearity of narrative in fiction, as well as through his darkly introspective vision of the labyrinth of modern—and modern Jewish—life.

Kafka was one in a long string of major Jewish cultural innovators writing in German to emerge out of central Europe in the late nineteenth century. Lacking full acceptance, these figures pushed many fields of European culture into new terrain, often adopting a critical sensibility that has been called "modernist." For example, Gustav Mahler demolished the composer Richard Wagner's biased assertion that Jews lacked all forms of musical creativity. Other figures such as Walter Benjamin (social criticism), Robert Musil (fiction), Max Reinhardt (theater), Arnold Schoenberg (music), and Franz Rosenzweig and Gershom Scholem (Jewish studies) broke new ground in their respective domains. Perhaps most significantly, Sigmund Freud defied established scientific views by developing the psychoanalytic method to probe the human subconscious. Freud was characteristic of many of this cohort in that he denied that there was anything distinctly Jewish to his work. At the same time, he did suggest to a colleague that there was a quality that fellow Jews possessed, a sort of "racial kinship," that allowed them to understand his psychoanalytic method better than non-Jews (specifically, Carl Jung).

Freud's comment suggests that an unspoken cultural and ethnic code existed among Jews of his day. It was not the religious beliefs and practices of Judaism that forged this code, but rather the social bonds borne of an environment in which Jews looked, spoke, and ate like their non-Jewish neighbors, but were still considered alien and even unwelcome in their home countries. Hannah Arendt juxtaposed the old fate of the Jews to the new by declaring that once they "had been able to escape from Judaism into conversion; from Jewishness there was no escape." The inescapability of Jewishness pointed to an irony of modern Jewish life, at least in central Europe—that the Enlightenment, with all its promise of liberation, could not deliver true freedom. The condition bred an iconoclastic spirit that had many brilliant cultural effects.

Central Europe was hardly the only or main site of Jewish cultural innovation. Neighboring eastern Europe hosted the largest population of Jews in the world, who created their own distinctive culture. In the more traditional and insular world of eastern Europe, Yiddish remained a dominant presence in the lives of Jews up to the twentieth century, whereas non-Jewish languages had by that time supplanted it as the main spoken tongues of Jews in central and western Europe and the Americas. Yiddish had served as a key language of religious instruction for the traditional-minded Jews of Eastern Europe; one notable example was the long-enduring *Tsenah u-renah* (Go forth and see) from the sixteenth century, a popular text intended for women that brought together a digest of the weekly Torah portion and various forms of supplications.

Beginning in the nineteenth century, as new political and cultural winds blew in from the West, a vibrant secular Yiddish literature began to emerge in the Russian Empire. Alongside parallel developments in other European literatures, Yiddish letters created new styles and genres, from low-brow fiction (known as *shund*) to high modernism to academic scholarly prose. Writers such as Mendele Moykher Sforim (Sh. Y. Abramowitch), Sholem Aleichem (Sh. Rabinovitz), and Y. L. Peretz mixed modern techniques, biting satire, and traditional sources to create a new Jewish literary canon in the late nineteenth and early twentieth centuries. Continuing in that tradition, the Polish-born Isaac Bashevis Singer, who emigrated to New York in 1935, wrote novels and stories in Yiddish marked by great poignancy and humor that earned him the Nobel Prize for Literature in 1978—the only writer in Yiddish to receive this honor.

The influence of Yiddish has been felt not only in fine literature. It became a multipurpose language of education, politics, economic activity, and a wide range of cultural expressions of which Jews in eastern Europe made extensive use, in addition to the language of the land. Moreover, Yiddish was a prominent linguistic presence in virtually every setting in which large numbers of its speakers resided, from Odessa to Amsterdam to New York to Melbourne. Of special note is its distinctive brand of humor that has informed the timing and locution of several generations of American Jewish comedians, including Sid Caesar, Woody Allen, Joan Rivers, Jerry Seinfeld, Sarah Silverman, and Jon Stewart. Well after Yiddish ceased to be the spoken language of hundreds of thousands of Jews on the Lower East Side of Manhattan, it lived and lives on through words and syntax that have entered American culture at large. At the same time, for the hundreds of thousands of strictly Orthodox *haredi* Jews who continue to speak Yiddish in America, Israel, and elsewhere, Yiddish comedy lives on in the form of the *badkhen*, the traditional bard-like figure who entertains at weddings and other happy occasions.

Perhaps even more dramatic than the revitalization of Yiddish in the nineteenth century was the appearance of a modern form of

4. Jewish girls peruse newspapers in both Yiddish and Polish in the reading room of a Jewish trade school. Jews in Poland between the two world wars were well known for speaking multiple languages. In the 1931 Polish census, nearly 80 percent declared Yiddish as their mother tongue, although most also spoke and read Polish, among other languages.

Hebrew, which had served to that point as the primary vehicle of Jewish scripture, liturgy, and law. This was not coincidental, since the two languages had a close and competitive relationship with one another. Hebrew played an important role in the *Haskalah* movement in late-eighteenth-century Berlin. It was both revered as the classic language of scripture and regarded as an essential agent for promoting Enlightenment ideals to the traditionally inclined. As the *Haskalah* movement expanded into eastern Europe via commercial and epistolary exchange, the function of Hebrew widened; its adepts recast it as a versatile modern language, suitable for the novel, essay form, literary journal, and scholarly monograph.

The revival of Hebrew as a modern language was intimately connected, in turn, to the revival of the dormant Jewish nation. In many nationalist movements, the motif of a people being awakened from slumber was common. Notwithstanding their lack of a territory of their own in which they dwelt (with the exception of a small number in Palestine), Jews were no different. In 1866, the Russian Hebrew poet Y. L. Gordon encapsulated the sentiment in a didactic poem:

> Awake, my people! How long will you slumber?
> The night has passed, the sun shines bright.
> Awake, lift up your eyes, look around you—
> Acknowledge, I pray you, your time and your place.

Later in the nineteenth century, eastern European Jewish intellectuals associated with the fledgling Zionist movement such as Ahad Ha'am, a leading Russian Jewish writer, transformed Hebrew into a vehicle for modern intellectual activity. In the twentieth century, when Zionism moved from its birthplace in Europe to Palestine, Hebrew became the language of the Jewish community there. Theodor Herzl, the founding father of political Zionism, was dubious that people would ever be able to ask for a railway ticket in Hebrew. But, in fact, the Holy Tongue became a living daily language, used to purchase railway tickets, negotiate with shopkeepers, and curse political opponents. In 1948 when the State of Israel was founded, Hebrew became the chief official language of the new country (alongside Arabic), with a state-sponsored language academy to guard its integrity.

With a measure of historical perspective, it can be argued that one of Zionism's greatest achievements was the transformation of Hebrew into a language spoken by millions *and* the creation of a world-class literary culture that has boasted outstanding prose writers and poets, including Yosef Hayim Brenner, Chaim Nahman Bialik, Rachel (Bluwstein), Leah Goldberg, S. Yizhar, Dahlia Ravikovitch, Yehuda Amichai, Amos Oz, and David Grossman. Validation of the excellence of Hebrew letters came in 1966 when one of the greatest of Israeli novelists, Shmuel Yosef Agnon, was awarded the Nobel Prize for Literature.

These literary figures were Jews of eastern or central European origin. They have been pillars of Jewish culture in Israel, and they often were closely connected to the Ashkenazi-dominated Labor Party establishment. Occupying a different space are Jews of Spanish and Middle Eastern origin, who have struggled to gain acceptance by the Ashkenazi political and cultural elite in the new state. Writers such as Eli Amir, Sami Michael, A. B. Yehoshua, Orly Castel-Bloom, Ronit Matalon, and Haim Sabato had and have accents, influences, and places of origin different from their Ashkenazi colleagues. They did not come from eastern or western Europe but rather from the Middle East. They grew up not with Yiddish, Russian, or German but rather Ladino (a prominent form of Judeo-Spanish), French, and Arabic. In fact, one of Israel's most accomplished Jewish authors, Samir Naqqash, won a wide and admiring audience throughout the Middle East for his literary work in the Arabic of his native Baghdad. In the musical realm, performers such as Zohar Argov, Haim Moshe, Yossi Banai, Haim, Ofra Haza, Eyal Golan, and Etty Akri have created an Israeli popular music that draws on the rhythms and tonality of the Arab world as much as on Western music. In the early twenty-first century, a number of well-known singers of Mizrahi origin, especially Kobi Oz and Ehud Banai, have reached back into the repertoire of North African Jewish religious culture to set liturgical poetry (*piyut*) to new music.

This last development is part of the return to tradition in some Jewish quarters in Israel and elsewhere that serves as a reminder that the secular era does not flow in only one direction—away from religion. Religion has undergone several major transformations in the modern age; initially shunted to the margins, it has reemerged with new force in the public square.

Part of the explanation for this change is that religion, as a cultural form, changes and adapts in response to shifting historical circumstance. So too, Jewish culture, from its early monotheistic roots, has continually changed in response to shifting circumstances and locales. This accounts for the extraordinary range of Jewish religious and cultural practices found in communities from Asia to the Americas. This constant exposure to new settings has strengthened the cultural muscle that Jews built up over centuries. While it has not always led to warm social relations with the non-Jewish population, this exposure has enabled Jews to develop effective tools of adaptation. Along the way, Jews have illustrated through their history how a minority culture can survive in the midst of an often hostile majoritarian society.

Chapter 4
Politics

When Aristotle famously declared in his *Politics* that "man is by nature a political animal," he thought of the capacity of humans to distinguish between right and wrong and good and bad. This quality was not only valuable for the individual, but was a key ingredient, he thought, in making both a household and a city-state.

While often lacking a state, Jews have been decidedly political animals throughout their history. They have demonstrated the ability to leverage the assets they possess to frame a strong sense of communal identity, as well as to thrive in challenging environments.

Some have suggested that the fact that Jews did not have sovereignty for two thousand years meant that they did not have a political history at all. This claim cannot be sustained. Jews had a rich political history, both in their homeland and in the diaspora, in their own state and beyond. To be sure, earlier eras demanded of the Jews a more muted and subordinate political voice compared to the modern age, but Jews constantly refined the skills of negotiation and accommodation through interactions with political powers in ancient and medieval times. And while they may not have had a state of their own, they linked their security and well-being to the fortunes of states, which largely served them in good stead.

Meanwhile, the modern era enabled a wider range of Jewish political expressions and deeds than ever seen before. A key point of entry into the modern political universe was the debate over whether Jews should be accorded full rights of citizenship by the emerging nation states of Europe. Perhaps most famously, Count Clermont-Tonnerre, a young aristocratic delegate, asserted in the midst of a discussion in the French National Assembly over the emancipation of the Jews in 1789: "The Jews should be refused everything as a nation, but granted everything as individuals." To gain full entry to the enlightened French state, he insisted, Jews would have to undo the strong bonds that tied them to their co-religionists and to Judaism's traditional norms.

Clermont-Tonnerre's oft-quoted prescription elicited an array of responses over the course of the nineteenth century. Some Jews reacted by hastening their efforts to leave behind traces of their Jewishness in order to "pass" into the Gentile world. Others set out to negotiate between the demands of the new political order and the desire to retain some of their traditional habits and affiliations; they became active in the state-sponsored religious communities that were newly established. Still others railed against the structures of power that denied to Jews—and others— full equal rights. This latter group of Jews often supported radical change in their host countries and beyond, focusing on the downtrodden at large rather than on Jews in particular.

Meanwhile, by the end of the nineteenth century, a group of Jews began to question the reliance of Jews on Gentile hosts. They altered the rallying cry of Jewish activists from "emancipation" to "auto-emancipation," as the Russian-Jewish doctor Leon Pinsker titled his 1882 manifesto. It was time, Pinsker declared, for Jews to recognize that despite their dispersed condition, they were not merely a loose band of individuals, but a nation deserving of the respect incumbent on that status. The physician Pinsker went on to offer a striking diagnosis: Gentiles were afflicted with a disease, "Judeophobia," that made Jews strangers everywhere they dwelt. To overcome this fate, Pinsker and fellow Jewish nationalists proposed different schemes and sites. Some sought to solve the problem by fortifying the Jewish nation in the diaspora. Others focused their efforts on restoring the Jews to their ancient homeland in Palestine, a project that eventually lead to the establishment of the State of Israel in 1948.

That seminal event in the history of the Jews had many consequences, one of which was to bring to fulfillment the long-standing hope of a return to the homeland. The aspiration to return was connected to the restoration of political sovereignty, which, traditionally, was linked to the coming of the Messiah—in line with the Talmudic declaration that "there is no difference between the present world and the messianic days other than an end to political subjugation." Although many leading Zionists eschewed traditional religious sensibilities, and even saw their movement as a renunciation of them, their vision of a reborn Jewish state was wrapped in grand historical and even messianic terms. That said, they would no longer wait for a messiah figure to redeem them, instead choosing to take action themselves to change the course of Jewish history.

The Zionist effort to restore Jewish sovereignty in the homeland was one of the main threads in the history of Jewish politics, but not the only one. Jewish politics in a broader sense also includes the kind of ongoing social adaptation that Jews undertook to ever-changing circumstances, frequently in settings in which they were a small minority. In those cases, Jews sought not sovereignty, but often a narrower form of communal autonomy. To gain a clearer picture of the range of Jewish political activity, this chapter will explore three defining relationships that have engaged and left a deep imprint on Jews as political actors.

Jews and the community

Because of their sparse numbers, the Jews had to make utmost use of their political skills. They parlayed their economic utility and cultural versatility into a grant of toleration that allowed them to maintain a rich communal life. A key to their success was knowing how to position themselves within a triangle of power of which they were one leg, along with the sovereign and the general populace. Typically, they aligned themselves with the ruling regime, mindful of the fact that there were clear benefits, as well as risks. Nevertheless, over the course of centuries, Jews' recourse to "vertical" or "royal" alliances with the ruling power was an effective strategy for guaranteeing their physical protection.

In the wake of the Holocaust, the political thinker Hannah Arendt questioned whether, in the Nazi era, this alliance had turned from a source of security to a writ of execution for Jews, who were lulled into excessive dependence on the state and went passively to their deaths. Many have challenged Arendt's sharp claim, suggesting that nothing in their previous experience could have prepared Jews for the genocidal nature of Nazism.

Indeed, it is instructive to see that premodern sovereigns, who belonged to competing religions, were prepared to guarantee the survival of the Jews and accord them control over their religious affairs. One might have expected that the tradition of granting latitude to Jewish religious observance under Babylonians, Greeks, and Romans would have come to an end with the rise of Christianity, given its vexed relationship with Judaism. In fact, Christian rulers largely continued and at times even expanded the practice of allowing Jews to regulate their communal and religious affairs.

That would have been impossible were it not for a major theological innovation by Church Fathers in the fourth century. The question they faced was simple enough: how to justify the survival of the Jews in light of the fact that they were held culpable for the ultimate capital crime—the death of Jesus.

St. Augustine developed his view of the Jews as a "witness people," whose dispersion and debasement reflected their rejection by God, but who should be kept alive as witnesses to the truth inhering in the Old Testament. Once it was determined that allowing the Jews to survive was theologically acceptable and even necessary, Church officials had to pair their desire to convert them with the obligation to protect them. For example, Pope Gregory the Great, who served from 590 to 604, issued a famous edict that declared that the Jews "ought to suffer no prejudice" and, in fact, could not be forcibly baptized, even though he and his successors fervently hoped for their conversion. As keepers of the Church's orthodoxy, popes were more likely to uphold this restrained principle of tolerance than the Christian rank and file, which was more inclined to act on its enmity in violent ways. Here too was a version of the triangle of power insofar as Jews dwelt between the strictures of Church doctrine and the sensibilities of their local neighbors.

This status required them to develop a prudent and savvy attitude toward the non-Jewish world. They did not have the luxury of cutting themselves off completely from that world; their very economic survival depended on extensive interaction. Conversely, their commercial skills, contacts, and acumen were valued by non-Jewish rulers. Christian sovereigns in medieval Europe invited Jews into their realm, granting them special charters, or "privilegia," that spelled out their rights and obligations to the sovereign. The charters granted a good deal of internal autonomy to Jews. On this basis, the designated leaders of the community, both lay and rabbinic, could regulate the religious and economic affairs of the community with relatively little interference from the outside. That is not to say that relations were always harmonious within the community—for example, between rabbis and businessmen, or even within either of those groups. But Jews for the most part managed their own affairs quite well, boasting their own executive and judicial bodies that oversaw most communal matters.

It is striking to see how committed some medieval Christian sovereigns were to the welfare of Jews in their realm. One of the most far-reaching examples comes from Duke Boleslaus of Greater Poland, who issued a charter in 1264 known as the Statute of Kalisz. The statute not only provided for the settlement of Jews in his realm, but also offered extensive protections to them, including a fine on Christians who failed to heed the cries of Jews in the middle of the night as well as a prohibition on municipal officials from intervening in the affairs of the *kehilah*.

Versions of the *kehilah* were found throughout the entire Jewish world, from the *judería* in medieval Spain to the *ghetto* of early modern Venice to the Jewish *millet* in the Ottoman Empire. And yet, it was in eastern Europe that communal autonomy reached its most developed form. Although regarded in modern times as the site of unremitting hostility—because of a string of violent outbreaks on its soil culminating in the Holocaust—eastern Europe was a far more multidimensional home to Jews. Not only were they able to build strong local communities, but they also created, beginning in the sixteenth century, regional federations of communities to represent their expanding interests. The largest and most successful example was the Council of Four Lands (Greater Poland, Little Poland, Ruthenia, and Volhynia). The council arose out of the annual market in Lublin, Poland, where merchants assembled, joined by Jewish jurists who came to discuss and adjudicate legal matters that could not be resolved at the local level and required a higher court of appeal. Over the course of its nearly two centuries of existence, the council featured both a supreme court and a legislative assembly that met at the markets at Lublin and the Galician city of Yaroslav. From the perspective of the Polish kingdom, the council's regional reach made it, at least for a time, a more effective organ of tax collection than appealing to a large number of individual *kehilot* (communities). With the development of a more centralized state apparatus in the eighteenth century, however, the utility of the council diminished, and it ceased to exist in 1764.

Some enemies of the Jews came to see the council as "a nation within a nation"—and thus as conclusive proof that Jews were capable of loyalty only to their own, and not to the host government. Meanwhile, Jewish nationalists in the twentieth century regarded the council as a model of inspiration. They sought to recapture the spirit of collective cohesion that premodern Jewish life possessed, while asserting more aggressively the need for Jews to take control of their own fate. For Diasporist nationalists such as Simon Dubnow, Yisroel Efroikin, and Vladimir Medem, the goal was two-staged: first, to acknowledge and fortify the very idea of a Jewish nation; and second, to create a realm of "national cultural autonomy" within the framework of an existing state in which Jewish linguistic, cultural, and educational norms would reign. Most advocates of this form of nationalism had in mind a Yiddish-speaking enclave in eastern Europe where the largest number of Jews in the world lived. In the period following the First World War, a number of political parties and even government ministries (for example, in Lithuania) were founded to promote the ideal of Jewish autonomy. During that time, the newly established Soviet Union conceived of and then established in 1934 a Jewish Autonomous Region in Birobidzhan close to the Russian-Chinese border. This concept of a Soviet Yiddish autonomous center never succeeded in drawing the masses, although it did attract a small number of Jews from around the world. That said, the ideal of an autonomous Jewish enclave in the diaspora has continued to excite literary imaginations, animating the work of writers such as Philip Roth in *Operation Shylock* (1993), in which a fictional protagonist named Philip Roth advances a doctrine called "Diasporism" that encourages Jews to leave Israel to return to their diaspora homes, and Michael Chabon in *The Yiddish Policemen's Union* (2007), whose setting is a Yiddish-speaking enclave of Jewish cultural autonomy in modern-day Alaska.

Although they did not develop a successful and long-standing example of Jewish cultural autonomy, Jews did endeavor to foster strong communal institutions in the modern age. The emancipatory bargain that Count Clermont-Tonnerre attempted to strike—citizenship rights in exchange for a diminution of Jewish group affiliation—did not suppress their longstanding communal impulse altogether. Moreover, European nations in the nineteenth century, especially those with a recognized state religion, often allowed for representative bodies to serve on behalf of religious communities. In the Jewish case, such centralized bodies as the French *consistoire* or the German *Gemeinde* could draw dues from and maintain some measure of discipline over their members, although still considerably less than the medieval *kehilah*.

Vestiges of this institutional model survived into the twentieth century in the form of the British Board of Deputies and Jewish Leadership Council, the French CRIF, and the German Zentralrat; similarly, beyond the European continent bodies such as the Argentine AMIA and DAIA, the Australian ECAJ, and the South African Board of Deputies could be found. By contrast, the pattern of centralized and often state-sponsored communal leadership that prevailed in Europe never took hold in the United States, where the joint traditions of disestablishment of religion and voluntary associations dominated. In the United States, a large and influential Jewish community did arise, but it was never represented by an official or single institutional body. Rather, the community was made up of a thick web of local, regional, and national organizations, among the most prominent of which were the American Jewish Committee, the Anti-Defamation League, B'nai B'rith, and the Hadassah/Women's Zionist Organization.

Jews and the state

Just as Jews have been able to preserve a strong measure of communal identity over centuries, so too they have constantly sought out and aligned themselves with state power. In fact, the two developments are closely connected, since Jews have almost always required state support and authorization to constitute their communities.

This reliance is one of the main facets of the long relationship between Jews and the state. The other is the Jews' own quest for state sovereignty, which has a long history. The origins of this latter impulse extend back to the late eleventh and early tenth centuries BCE, when the institution of kingship was introduced in ancient Israel. Saul, the first king of Israel, had a tense relationship with his son-in-law, David, whom he had once tried to kill. Upon ascending the throne, David moved the capital of the fledgling Israelite kingdom from Hebron to Jerusalem. David was said to have many talents—as giant-slayer, warrior, poet, musician, unifier of the tribes. But because he had spilled so much blood in battle, he was not permitted, according to the Bible, to build a suitable edifice to house the Ark of the Covenant that contained the Ten Commandments. That task fell to his second son, Solomon, who built the Holy Temple in Jerusalem.

The completion of the Temple in the mid-tenth century created a major new Israelite cult shrine, although it was not the only Israelite shrine in Palestine. Local sites of sacrifice were spread throughout the country. Over time, the Temple's reach expanded, and it became a chief destination for religious pilgrims outside of Jerusalem, especially after the destruction of the northern kingdom of Israel by the Assyrians in 722 BCE. The subsequent period was marked by internal dissension and external threat from a variety of local powers. It also featured the increasingly bold voice of Israelite prophets, who offered both hope and admonition over Israel's sins up to—and then after—the destruction of the Temple in 586 BCE.

Thus came to an end the first period of Israelite sovereignty, which yielded to an era of "diaspora politics" in which there was not a single center. From that point forward, the desire to return to the land, rebuild the Holy Temple, and restore Israelite kingship became a matter of daily recitation and fervently held prayers. This ambition was partly realized during the time of the Hasmonean dynasty in the second and first centuries BCE, followed by the Romans' Jewish vassal king, Herod. The subsequent destruction of the Second Temple reignited the aspiration for sovereignty. But for much of late antique and medieval times, that desire floated on a distant and otherworldly plane of time, in contrast to the everyday needs and expectations that shaped the Jews' sense of the present. According to that second domain of time, sovereignty was a far-off goal. The tangible short-term objective was communal autonomy for a minority living under majority rule. This more limited quest did *not* entail an absence of politics. On the contrary, Jews were able to make use of the political wisdom they had accrued from the time of their exile in Babylonia to safeguard their self-interests by aligning with the state.

Of course, the alliance with state power was not infallible. The fact that Jews, because of their particular and exacting rituals, received certain dispensations that other groups did not made them the targets of hostility and periodic violence. One notorious instance was in Alexandria in 38 CE, when lingering resentment by both Egyptian and Greek residents of the city toward Jews, fueled by the agitation of the local governor, Flaccus, broke out into violent riots. The prominent philosopher Philo subsequently wrote a condemnation of him, *Against Flaccus*, that made clear that this episode was an exception to the rule of peaceable relations between diaspora Jews and their ancient hosts. At the same time, the episode highlighted the vulnerabilities Jews experienced as part of the complex triangle of power.

Arrayed against those vulnerabilities were the extensive protections that local and regional rulers granted Jews under both medieval Christendom and Islam. In addition to the charters of Christian sovereigns, Muslim rulers adopted a policy of measured toleration toward Jews. An important early affirmation came in the Constitution of Medina, a pact forged by Muhammad in 622 CE. The constitution was an attempt by the Muslim prophet to assure peaceable relations among warring groups, including Jewish tribes, in the Arabian Peninsula. Among its clauses were several that guaranteed non-Muslims the same political rights as Muslims, as well as according them religious autonomy. These principles were reiterated in the Pact of Umar, a legal document of uncertain provenance, that came to regulate relations between Muslim rulers and non-Muslim "protected people" or *dhimmi*, including Jews. Under its terms, Muslim rulers were obligated to provide protection and allow religious autonomy to those *dhimmi* who upheld the pact. At the same time, it enumerated a number of restrictions on Jews and Christians, including the prohibition on building new houses of worship and the obligation to maintain a deferential attitude toward Muslims and Islam. Over time, Muslim rulers also required *dhimmi* to pay a special poll tax known as the *jizyah*. This kind of contractual relationship reflected the status of Jews as a tolerated, but subservient religious minority in the Middle Ages, under both Muslim and Christian regimes. To be sure, there was considerable variation, both between Christian and Muslim regimes and within each. Actual living conditions depended on a mix of factors—the temperament of the ruler, the mood of the populace, the economic climate of the day, and even the presence of influential Jewish court advisors who lobbied on behalf of their community.

If medieval sovereigns evinced varying degrees of *toleration* for the Jews, the hope arose that a new political principle, *equality*, would become the hallmark of modern regimes. Jews believed that they had amply demonstrated the trust required to earn rights of citizenship, although the charge of "dual loyalty" frequently arose. To assure himself on this account, the newly declared French emperor Napoleon Bonaparte convened in 1806 a distinguished group of Jews in Paris, posing to them a set of questions intended to determine whether the deepest affinities of Jews lay with the French or the Jewish collective. The group, which was named the Paris Sanhedrin in evocation of the great ancient body of sages, responded in somewhat convoluted but positive terms. For example, it affirmed that a Jew could marry a Christian under French civil law, and that the bonds of loyalty to the fatherland, France, were stronger than those between two Jews of differing nationalities. To a great extent, the Sanhedrin's formulations marked a decisive inversion whereby halakhah assumed a position of secondary significance to civil law in the lives of Jews.

This inversion signaled, in turn, the Jews' enthusiastic devotion to the states of which they were now or soon to become citizens. In general, one of the central lessons of their long journey through history—at least up to the twentieth century—was that the alliance with state power, with all its vagaries, was the best bet for security and well-being. This was one of the reasons why major Jewish financiers such as the Pintos, Rothschilds, Warburgs, Sassoons, and Loebs invested heavily in the economies and governments of the countries in which they lived.

Challenges to this historical lesson inevitably appeared. One of the most notorious examples was the "Dreyfus Affair" of 1894 in which a French army officer who happened to be Jewish, was falsely accused of espionage for the hated Germans. The rapidly escalating uproar surrounding Captain Dreyfus provoked the French masses on both side of the issue, pro-Dreyfusards and anti-Dreyfusards, to give loud voice to their opinion about whether Jews were capable of loyalty to their state. Observing the unfolding spectacle on the Paris streets was a visiting Jewish journalist from Vienna, for whom it was unimaginable that here in the French capital, where the first decree of Jewish emancipation was granted in 1790, crowds were chanting "death to the Jews." The sight shocked the journalist, an assimilated Jew named Theodor Herzl, who previously had considered leading a group of Jewish children to the baptismal font as a reflection of his belief in the virtues of full social integration. Beholding the angry masses on the streets, Herzl now came to the conclusion that Europe was no longer hospitable to Jews. In a feverish pitch in 1896, he authored a short pamphlet in German called *The Jewish State* (or more accurately, *The State of the Jews*) that called for Jews to take control of their own historical destiny and leave Europe to create a state of their own. One year later, Herzl organized and presided over the first Zionist Congress in Basel, Switzerland. At the end of that gathering in the summer of 1897, Herzl recorded in his diary that he had set in motion an inexorable process leading to the establishment of a state.

It took fifty-one years for a Jewish state to come into existence. During that period, Zionists of many different stripes—socialist, religious, left-wing, and right-wing, among others—expounded their vision of what a Jewish national society in Palestine should look like. By the second decade of the twentieth century, the main focus of Zionist activity had shifted from Europe, where the World Zionist Organization was founded, to Palestine itself. Already by that point, Zionists had come to understand that the country of their dreams was inhabited by a large native Arab population that looked on with growing suspicion at the arrival of the new Jewish settlers. Tensions over land, labor, and overall political aims rose between Jews and Arabs, each of which regarded itself as the true heir of the ancient land. Following a particularly explosive conflagration at the Western Wall in 1929, in the wake of which more than one hundred Jews were killed by Arab rioters, Zionist leaders homed in with new intensity on the goal of creating a Jewish state in Palestine with a Jewish majority. This aim gained particular urgency in the 1930s, with the rise to power of Adolf Hitler in Germany and his increasingly realistic plans to rid the world of Jews. In the face of that grave threat, the leader of the

Zionists in Palestine, David Ben-Gurion, had to make difficult choices about where to allocate the limited resources at his disposal. He exhibited a combination of steely resolve, ideological commitment, and strategic pragmatism in guiding Zionism to the realization of its goals.

A huge step toward that objective came with the vote by the United Nations General Assembly on November 29, 1947, to partition Palestine into Jewish and Arab states. The Zionists accepted the vote, while the local Arab population and neighboring Arab countries rejected it and the underlying premise of partition. They could not imagine surrendering a majority of the land of Palestine to a group of recent arrivals that

5. Jews throughout the world, though especially those in Palestine, greeted news of United Nations General Assembly Resolution 181 on November 29, 1947 with great celebration. The resolution called for the partition of Palestine into Arab and Jewish states, which Zionists regarded as definitive international recognition of their claim to sovereignty.

6. In the midst of the armed struggle between Jews and Arabs in 1948, Palestinians took flight and sometimes were expelled from their homes in towns and cities such as Jaffa. They tried to bring with them whatever possessions they could as they fled to neighboring countries, such as Jordan, Lebanon, and Syria, where many of their descendants remain as refugees to this day.

amounted to one-third of the population. Ben-Gurion, for his part, took no time to celebrate the UN decision, assuming that armed hostilities were not far away. And indeed, already in early December, local Arab attacks commenced in Jerusalem, soon to break out into a wider conflict between Jewish and Arab forces in the next year. The war of 1948 passed through various stages: a first phase between local Arab and Jewish forces; and a second phase, after the Zionist leadership proclaimed the State of Israel on May 14, 1948, when the armies of neighboring Arab states invaded.

The various rounds of battle led to two dramatic and intertwined results. First, the Zionists, fighting what they saw as a war of survival, gained the upper hand and achieved independence for

7. In June 1967, Israel won a quick and overwhelming victory over Arab states, following which it came to occupy new territories, including the West Bank, where it initially placed army posts and then civilian settlers. In September 1967, Israeli prime minister Levi Eshkol and defense minister Moshe Dayan took a helicopter tour of the new army installations in the West Bank.

the new State of Israel. The result was dramatic: the restoration of political sovereignty to the Jews in their homeland after two thousand years. Jews the world over, including many who were agnostic or even hostile to Zionism before, now expressed joy at this epochal event. The stakes of the war in Palestine were particularly high, coming a few short years after the murder of millions of Jews in the Holocaust. The newly created state quickly became a magnet for Jewish immigrants in need, both Holocaust survivors and Jews displaced from Arab lands. For these Jews, the arc of their life journey had curved from exile to homeland. More broadly, Jews had regained control over their collective fate.

A second major outcome of the 1948 war moved in the opposite direction. In the course of fighting, it is estimated that more than 700,000 Palestinian Arabs fled or were expelled from their homes in what they referred to as the *Nakba* (catastrophe). This event was a searing and defining moment in Palestinian national consciousness. The ongoing legacy of this displacement is the presence of millions of Palestinian refugees outside of Israel/Palestine who remain at the core of the ongoing conflict between Jews and Arabs to this day. While this conflict has not prevented Israel from growing into a powerful and technologically advanced society, its perpetuation may well pose a substantial political, economic, and moral burden on the Jewish state in the future. In similar fashion, Israel's conquest of territory with a large Palestinian population in the 1967 Six-Day War, particularly the West Bank of the Jordan River, has led to an ongoing occupation that endangers the long-standing Zionist ideal of a Jewish state with a Jewish majority.

Jews and the self

To the extent that Jews had an active political life prior to 1948, it came about not through a state of their own but rather in small communities embedded in non-Jewish regimes. It may well be that the dispersion of Jews in these communities the world over, instead of being concentrated in a single country, was an important factor in their survival.

Much of Jewish political activity has been devoted to the preservation of the *collective*. But this work would have been unimaginable without the active intervention and guidance of *individuals*. In the case of Zionism, the ambition of reviving the Jewish nation in Palestine required the skill and vision of individuals, ranging from the founding ideological forefathers, Theodor Herzl, Ahad Ha-am, and Nachman Syrkin, to committed implementers, such as David Ben-Gurion, Berl Katznelson, Golda Meir, and Chaim Weizmann.

Individuals served as key interlocutors on behalf of communal interests much earlier in Jewish history. The Hebrew prophets, beginning with the towering Moses and moving forward to Amos,

Isaiah, and Jeremiah, among others, mediated between human and divine realms, striving to translate God's imperatives into graspable terms. They insisted that their audience, the children of Israel, pursue justice as a fulfillment of the principle that human beings were crafted in God's image. Their charge that "Justice, justice, thou shall pursue" survived well past the end of prophecy, becoming an important inspiration for Jewish social activism, often of a manifestly secular nature, in Europe and the United States in the twentieth and twenty-first centuries.

Meanwhile, the Middle Ages pushed to prominence the role of the Jewish intercessor with the non-Jewish world. In Muslim Spain, the figure of the court Jew came on the scene. The Jewish courtier was often a man of substantial means, fluent in multiple languages, conversant in a dizzying array of intellectual topics (from poetry to astrology), and closely aligned to the king. Court Jews performed the double task of acting as trusted advisors to the sovereign and as representatives of the interests of the Jewish community with the court. This figure also played an important role in central Europe between the sixteenth and eighteenth centuries. Some scholars suggest that early modern court Jews, through their money-lending and banking capacities, played a key role in the rise of the modern nation-state, for example, by helping to finance the new institution of a regular standing army that could assure constancy of support for the regime. At the same time, because of their close ties to the sovereign, court Jews could become targets of resentment and hatred from an angry populace. One especially well known court Jew, the early-eighteenth-century financier Joseph Süß Oppenheimer, was so loathed for alleged corruption and tax gouging that, on the death of his patron, in 1737, the Duke of Württemberg, he was immediately arrested and subsequently executed. The Nazi propagandist Joseph Goebbels seized on the story and arranged for the production of a movie based on Oppenheimer, "Jud Süß," that became one of the most notorious pieces of anti-Semitic agitation in modern times.

The court Jew of early modern Europe was one variant of a broader vocation of Jewish intercession known by the Hebrew term *shtadlanut* (whose practitioner was a *shtadlan*). The *shtadlan* promoted the interests of the Jewish community with the sovereign, ensuring that taxes be paid promptly and, concomitantly, that the promised protections and autonomy be provided. *Shtadlanim* were communal liaisons who came to be trusted precisely because they and fellow Jews were deemed to have no political aspirations of their own, that is, no desire to establish their own state, and thus were able to pledge full loyalty to the sovereign. Although most who filled this role were men, perhaps the best known court Jew of all was a woman, Doña Gracia (Mendes) Nasi, who was born a Christian in Portugal in 1510, reclaimed her family's Jewish heritage after leaving her home country, and ended her life as a wealthy businesswoman and enormously influential communal leader at the Sultan's court in Ottoman Turkey.

Early modern court Jews performed a range of important functions. They also marked out, through their behavior, the advent of a new attitude and comportment that can be called modern. In the pursuit of their assignments, which often included socializing at court, they could be less scrupulously observant in upholding Jewish law than the rest of their co-religionists. The license they may have taken in indulging in non-kosher food or drink, for example, was justified in the name of performing communal service. The new liberty of the court Jew highlights a broader trend: the desire of Jews in the eighteenth century to make their way out of the tight-knit and inward-looking *kehilah*. By modifying the social and ritual practices of Jews, the court Jews opened the door to the outside world and, as one notable scholar wrote, "prepared the way for a new era."

This era was marked by a new emphasis on the individual. Up to this point, the focus has been on individuals working on behalf of the Jewish collective, from prophets to court Jews. The modern

era upended the priorities of previous epochs, transforming the individual's well-being into an end in itself. This was not solely or even primarily due to the fact that some court Jews slipped from full observance into a more lax state. It was a pillar of the new Enlightenment worldview that placed great emphasis on the rational faculties of individuals. The new political theory that accompanied this belief regarded the individual no longer as a tolerated subject, but rather as the citizen of a state to whom both rights and responsibilities devolved.

Jews, who had been constantly placed at the margins of Christian European society, were now included in this vision but on the condition that they surrender, as Clermont-Tonnerre demanded, a good portion of their communal identity. One French Jewish leader of the day, Beer Isaac Beer from Lorraine, internalized this demand when he urged his fellow Jews in 1791 to "divest ourselves entirely of that narrow spirit, of Corporation and Community, in all civil and political matters."

Beer's call points to one of the great challenges of the Jews' entry into modernity: how to realize the benefits of the new individualism without abandoning their Jewish roots altogether? This was a challenge of which Beer's German contemporary, Moses Mendelssohn, was keenly aware. In the face of constant calls to convert, Mendelssohn steadfastly held on to his scrupulous Jewish observance. And yet his observance was different from that of his forebears in one regard: it rested on a view of religion as a matter of rational choice rather than of rote obligation or coercion.

8. Doña Gracia Nasi Mendes was one of the most powerful Jews in the sixteenth century. Born into a Roman Catholic family that had been forcibly converted from Judaism in Portugal, she then "returned" to Judaism, using her business acumen and wealth to support other Jews (and especially other former *conversos*) to excape the scrutiny of the Inquisition in Antwerp, Venice, and Ferrara, Italy. Eventually, she made her way to the Ottoman Empire, where she joined forces with her nephew and son-in-law, Don Joseph Nasi, to continue her business and charitable activities.

Consistent with this view, Mendelssohn did not believe that rabbis should have the power of excommunication. Jews should be free to think and practice as they choose, indeed, to exert their personal autonomy.

Mendelssohn's life and thought left behind a complicated legacy. At the most personal level, his mix of ritual observance and commitment to personal autonomy proved to be a difficult balance to uphold for his family; four of six of his children ended up converting to Christianity. In terms of intracommunal politics, his challenge to the supremacy of rabbinic authority coaxed into existence the early-nineteenth-century movement to reform Judaism, which then triggered the reactions that led to the rise of Orthodox and Conservative (or Positive-Historical) Judaism. These denominational camps would leave a deep imprint on modern Jewish life, especially in the United States. Meanwhile, Mendelssohn's advocacy for full civic rights for Jews inspired several generations of Jewish political activists in Europe ranging from the Polish-born Frenchman Zalkind Hourwitz to the German activists Gabriel Riesser and Ludwig Börne. Whereas Hourwitz's France granted Jews rights in 1790–1791, it was not until 1871 that Jews gained full political emancipation in Mendelssohn's native German lands.

The staggered pace of emancipation had a good deal to do with the political map of Europe in the nineteenth century, which was redrawn on numerous occasions, for example, after the Congress of Vienna (1815) and the Franco-Prussian War (1870–1871). It also had to do with Europe's lingering ambivalence toward the Jew. Even when Jews had gotten rid of "the narrow spirit of Corporation and Congregation," even when they had abandoned the language, rites, and dress of their pious forebears, they were often received with skepticism and lack of warmth. Caught between worlds old and new, European Jews adopted a variety of strategies, ranging from conversion to renewed religious commitment to political radicalism.

Those who adopted this last path sought to translate the historical experience of Jews as a persecuted minority into a commitment to a more equitable society for all. Perhaps the most significant critic of the injustices of society was Karl Marx, born a Jew and baptized as a child, who agitated in the latter half of the nineteenth century for a sweeping human emancipation that would overturn the existing economic and political orders. Marx spawned several generations of radicals, who included prominent Jews such as Kurt Eisner, Rosa Luxemburg, and Leon Trotsky in Europe as well as Abe Cahan, Emma Goldman, and, later, Gus Tyler in the United States. Brandishing this commitment to fight injustice, Jews became important allies of African Americans in the civil rights struggle in the United States; leaders in this struggle ranged from the wealthy businessman Julius Rosenwald in the early part of the century to the legendary Rabbi Abraham Joshua Heschel in the 1960s. So too in the anti-apartheid struggle in South Africa, Jews including Ronald Kasrils, Albie Sachs, and Joe Slovo played prominent leadership roles. In related fashion, Jewish women initiated and led movements devoted to women's rights, from the Germans Bertha Pappenheim and Regina Jonas in the early twentieth century to the Americans Betty Friedan, Gloria Steinem, Sally Priesand, and Blu Greenberg in the late twentieth century.

This roster of figures makes clear that not all modern Jews imagined themselves as close allies of the state; rather, some chose to swim against the current of establishment politics. But given their historical proclivity for the "royal alliance," it should come as no surprise that Jews have distinguished themselves in positions of political leadership in Europe, the United States, and elsewhere. A highly selective list of Jewish state officials includes Benjamin Disraeli (nineteenth-century British prime minister,) Matthew Nathan and Herbert Samuel (British colonial officials), Louis Brandeis (early-twentieth-century U.S. Supreme Court justice), Walter Rathenau (early-twentieth-century German foreign minister), Léon Blum and Pierre Mendès-France (twentieth-century French prime ministers), Ana Pauker (mid-twentieth-century Romanian foreign minister), John Key (New Zealand prime minister from 2008), Madeleine Albright (late-twentieth-century U.S secretary of state), Helen Suzman (long-standing South African parliamentarian), André Azoulay (senior advisor to the royal court of Morocco), Joseph Lieberman (U.S. senator and candidate for vice president in 2000), and Bernie Sanders (U.S. senator and candidate for president in 2016).

These individuals continued the long-standing Jewish practice of investing hope in the possibility of positive change through the state. To one side of them were the Jewish rebels who devoted their lives to fighting the inequality found in established states; and to the other side were those who felt as strangers in a Gentile world and aimed to establish a self-standing Jewish state. The path of the latter group, the Zionists, led to the attainment of sovereignty, an act that has served as an anchor of Jewish political life in the twentieth and twenty-first centuries. Indeed, the state of Israel has not only been home to its citizens; it has also become a source of pride, attention, and support for Jews who choose not, or are unable, to immigrate to it. Israel's symbols and leaders—from Ben-Gurion to Menachem Begin to Yitzhak Rabin—were and are revered in much of the Jewish world. In that regard, association with the sovereign state of Israel has become a prominent—and in many circles, dominant—form of Jewish identity, even for those who live beyond the country's borders.

At the same time, modern Jewish life revolves around another axis of sovereignty, one that is the natural outgrowth of Moses Mendelssohn's vision of autonomy. It is what a pair of Jewish scholars, Steven Cohen and Arnold Eisen, called in 2000 "the sovereign self," referring to the typical Jewish individual who decides on her life path without excessive fealty to the weight of the past or to established communal institutions. This form of "sovereignty" rests on the proposition that there are many portals, not just one, through which to enter into Jewishness—and that the decision rests entirely in the hands of the individual.

The contrast between these two forms of sovereignty is striking. One is rooted in Israel, the other in the diaspora, especially in North America; they represent the two main demographic and political centers in the Jewish world. One emphasizes a collective vision of identity and speaks in defense of communal obligation, whereas the other heralds the individual and his right to personal autonomy.

And yet, this contrast between communal and individual politics should not be overstated. After all, the American Jewish community, where the culture of personal autonomy has sunk deep roots, has also been an exceptionally strong supporter of Israel within the American political system, in which it exerts an influence well beyond its numbers. Whether that advocacy will continue as before—given shifting demographic currents in American Jewry and the growing drift between Jewish and Israeli political values over the Israeli-Palestinian conflict—remains an open question. Several outcomes are imaginable: it is possible that the tension between the two regnant forms of sovereignty will become more pronounced in coming decades. It is also possible that a deeper sense of the benefits of a mutually reinforcing relationship will develop, in line with Jewish philosopher Simon Rawidowicz's notion of an equal "partnership" between the two Jewish centers. And it is possible that a significant realignment in the balance of power will occur as Israel continues to grow demographically and North America declines. Whichever of those scenarios—or another—will prevail, it is important to note that the founding of the State of Israel and the growth of the North American Jewish community represent two of the most noteworthy chapters in the long political history of the Jews.

Chapter 5

Perceptions

By almost all reasonable measures, the Jews have had a remarkable historical journey. The length and challenges of that journey have instilled in them a pair of competing sensibilities: a frequent feeling of vulnerability, as if the next major crisis is around the corner; and a somewhat mythic feeling of invulnerability insofar as Jews have survived trials large and small for thousands of years. This latter sentiment should not obscure the fact that Jews are flesh and blood people, who have lived tangible lives filled with adventure, joy, and tragedy.

This rather banal point assumes greater significance when we recall that "Jews" have also been an idea, a construct crafted by non-Jews to perform various functions. In a 1988 book, the French philosopher Jean-François Lyotard juxtaposed real-life Jews to "the jews," emphasizing the lower case and plural form to connote the symbolic alien group that European society constantly constructed in order to attack or expel.

There is, in fact, a longer genealogy to this idea of the idea of the Jew. Spinoza hints at it in the seventeenth century in *A Theologico-Political Treatise* when he maintained that one of the key preservative forces of Jewish life was the "universal hate" of the Gentile. This notion of the Gentile construction of the Jew became even more explicit when antisemitism announced itself with aplomb in the last quarter of the nineteenth century. The mayor of Vienna from 1897 to 1910, Karl Lueger, who ran for office on an openly antisemitic platform, captured that brashness when responding to a question about why he had Jewish friends: "I decide," he provocatively declared, "who is a Jew."

A half century later, the French philosopher Jean-Paul Sartre provided a more tempered view of the phenomenon by which the antisemite defines the Jew. In *Réflexions sur la question juive* (1946; published in English as *Anti-Semite and Jew*), he identified the distinctive role that the Jew played as "the stranger, the intruder, the unassimilated at the very heart of our society." This status prompted Sartre to offer his own iconic definition of the Jew as "the one whom other men consider a Jew." More recently, the historian David Nirenberg has written a sweeping account in *Anti-Judaism* (2013) of how the idea of Judaism—or more accurately, opposition to it—has been an organizing principle of Western civilization.

This line of thought attests to the fact that the reputation of Jews far exceeds their numbers. While constituting a miniscule minority in virtually every society of which they have been part, they have been the source of persistent rumors, fears, allegations, and conspiracy theories. The resulting body of anti-Jewish expression has a certain spectral—and counterintuitive—quality, since it often has been formulated in the physical absence of Jews. Indeed, antisemitism reaches its highest rates, according to the 2014 Anti-Defamation League global survey, where the smallest percentage of Jews lives—for example, in the Middle East, where nearly 75 percent harbor antisemitic views, or in eastern Europe at 34 percent.

On what does this antipathy rest? What is it about Jews that haunts those among whom they dwell—and even more, those among whom they do not dwell? In response, it must be said that Jews not only have harbored a sense of their own uniqueness throughout their long history, but also have been disproportionately represented in a variety of domains that capture the attention of antisemites, including business, academia, and political activism. And yet, those factors still cannot explain the amount of mental energy and paranoia that goes into imagining the Jew as a nefarious force intent on global domination. This is the foundational pillar of the *Protocols of the Elders of Zion*, which has the dubious distinction of being the most popular piece of antisemitic literature ever written, having been disseminated in millions of copies. The *Protocols* was drafted in the early twentieth century as a purported set of transcripts of meetings of Jewish leaders intent on subverting the existing world order through a mix of capitalism and communism. This mix affords a bit of insight into the staying power of anti-Jewish expression. It is such that it can embrace opposite representations of the Jew—for example, arch capitalist and revolutionary communist, ultra-pious separatist and rootless cosmopolitan—in the same breath.

But again, why the Jews? Why have they, of all groups, merited this attention across time and space? And how did they manage to withstand it? The answers, as this book suggests, are interrelated. The Jews—or their precursors, the ancient Israelites—developed a sense of their chosenness at an early stage in their collective life. Later they spawned and posed a challenge to Christianity, which claimed that it had inherited the mantle of the true Israel—and came to regard latter-day Jews as stiff-necked and obsolete. Rather than fold and disappear in the face of this new movement, Jews persisted in their beliefs and practices, matching Christian claims of exceptionalism with their own. They combined a measure of theological contempt with recognition of the indispensability of interaction with the wider Gentile world. In the course of that interaction, they found new sources of economic sustenance and cultural expression, while also encountering incredulity and disappointment, especially in the Christian world, that they refused to surrender their way of life. The resulting hostility reaffirmed their own sense of difference, which then fed into renewed Gentile resentment and condemnation.

This was a complex cycle in which both parties, Jews and Gentiles, had agency. The Jews' chosenness and the Gentiles' inversion of it created friction. For much of their relationship, that friction was livable. The two sides dwelt together in the same cities and towns, gaining greater familiarity, exchanging cultural values, and at the same time, sharpening a sense of difference toward one another.

This relationship of mutual perception was fragile, but long-standing. In the twentieth century, two developments threatened to undo it. First, the flood of murderous violence unleashed in the Holocaust removed the largest population of Jews in the world from proximity to their Christian neighbors in eastern Europe. And second, Jews in North America achieved an unsurpassed level of acceptance that began to dissolve the social boundaries that separated Jew from Gentile.

And yet these two countervailing trends have not altogether shattered the age-old mutual perceptions. Even as Jews have assimilated into American and other Western societies, losing many traces of their forebears' distinctiveness, many have retained the fight against antisemitism as a defining credo of their existence. They have established organizations devoted to that fight, which also serve to fortify their own sense of identity. They have also devoted substantial time and resources to memorializing the Holocaust, especially as the generation of concentration camp survivors passes from the world. This work remains a top Jewish communal priority—and a key source of Jewish identity. In fact, in the Pew Research Center's 2013 *Portrait of Jewish Americans*, "remembering the Holocaust" was considered the most essential part of being Jewish. Meanwhile, for much of the Gentile world, the Jews (or per Lyotard, the "jews" as idea) remain an ongoing enigma after Auschwitz, alternately admired, resented, and reviled depending where and when one turns. Over the course of their history, Jews have indeed cast a powerful spell on the Gentile imagination, falling into different categories of offense that together make them a common target.

"A novel form of worship opposed to all that is practised by other men"

It was the Roman historian Tacitus who credited the biblical Moses with crafting "a novel form of worship" that differed from all others in his major chronicle of Rome, *The Histories*. Tacitus did not see the advent of Judaism as a salutary development. Rather, he was filled with the contempt Romans often had of foreigners when describing them; thus, practitioners of Judaism were wicked, lascivious, indolent, and beholden to rituals that were "sinister and revolting," particularly the practice of circumcision.

The notion that Judaism was distinct from other religions—and that its adherents were intent on keeping separate from the rest of society—preceded the Roman era. The earlier Greek historian Manetho (third century BCE) inveighed against the Jews' practices and behavior, as reported by Josephus.

And yet the perception of Jewish religious difference became a far more serious issue in the Christian era, especially given the claim that Jews were culpable for the death of Jesus Christ. Christian theologians, as was noted, did not recommend the Jews' eradication. But they were intent on demonstrating the superiority of Christianity. Jews, for their part, interpreted Christian enmity not as a refutation of their religion but as a trial whose end was the affirmation of their own religion.

This rivalry turned more heated as Christianity established its center in Europe in the early Middle Ages (fifth to tenth centuries CE). Jews shared among themselves a disparaging polemical work in Hebrew, *Toldot Yeshu* (The history of Jesus) that depicted Jesus as an illegitimate child who became a philandering faith-healer. Christians captured the nature of the relationship between the two religions in the statue "Ecclesia et Synagoga" (Church and Synagogue) that was placed on cathedrals throughout medieval Europe, including Notre Dame in Paris. The statue depicts two women figures, one, Ecclesia, who stands upright and looks ahead with crown on head and cross staff in hand; the other woman figure, Synagoga, has a bowed head, is blindfolded, has a broken staff in one hand and is losing control of a book of scripture in the other. In this stark contrast, Christianity is the source of vision, truth, and the future, whereas Judaism is broken, blind, and a vestige of the past.

The assertion of the theological inferiority of Judaism found ample visual and physicalized representation in medieval Christendom. Jews were depicted as devil-like, possessed of horns and a tail, and singularly intent on continuing to attack Jesus by desecrating the sacramental host wafer that represented Christ's body in Roman Catholic doctrine. Closely related was a range of descriptions of Jews as a female pig known as the *Judensau* and as beset by a foul smell distinct to them (graced with the Latin name *foetor Judaicus*). All of these images betray a degree of knowledge, even intimate knowledge, by Christians of Jewish habits—*and* a complete inversion of that knowledge. Thus, Jews' fastidious attention to hygiene and good health was converted into an assertion of their utter filth.

Images of the Jews' dirtiness assumed even more sinister form when blood entered into the story. The claim that Jews murdered Christian children to use their blood—for example, to prepare the unleavened bread eaten during Passover (*matsah*) or to poison wells—stood at the heart of the infamous blood libel whose origins extend back to the twelfth century in Norwich, England (1144). This accusation was destined for a long future, making hundreds of appearances in the Middle Ages. The modern era witnessed a new proliferation of ritual murder charges, perhaps most famously in Damascus, Syria, in 1840 when local Jews were accused of kidnapping and using the blood of an Italian monk for the preparation of *matsah* on Passover. Later in the century, the claim of murder by Jews for ritual purposes cropped up in both Hungary (1882) and Austria (1899). And in the early twentieth century, a Russian Jew named Mendel Beilis was accused of ritual murder of a Christian child in Kiev in 1913. The case of Beilis, who was acquitted of the charges, was memorialized fifty years later in Bernard Malamud's novel *The Fixer* (1966).

Blood-based allegations against Jews endure to this day, especially in the Arab and Muslim worlds (where Jews are largely absent, although a frequent target of vilification). Former Egyptian president Muhamad Morsi made reference in a 2010 interview to Zionists as "bloodsuckers" and "descendants of apes and pigs." In 2015, a website run by an Iranian parliamentarian referred to the Jews as "history's most bloodthirsty people." Meanwhile, in the United States, Louis Farrakhan, leader of the Nation of Islam, pronounced this judgment on American Jews in 1996:

> You are wicked deceivers of the American people. You have sucked their blood. You are not real Jews, those of you that are not real Jews. You are the synagogue of Satan, and you have wrapped your tentacles around the U.S. government, and you are deceiving and sending this nation to hell.

The leap from the original charge of deicide to allegations of the uncleanliness of Jews to their putative quest for blood indicates the snaking, inconsistent, and tenacious nature of anti-Jewish expression. It also reveals how earlier claims based on religion served as the foundation for other sorts of charges that cast Jews as an almost mystical and demonic force.

"Money is the jealous God of Israel"

Karl Marx's notorious assertion that "money is the jealous God of Israel," drawn from his essay "On the Jewish Question" (1844), foregrounds another deep-seated perception of Jews as unfailingly avaricious and acquisitive. Some have pointed to Marx's background as a baptized Jew to suggest that he was filled with self-loathing—and thus game to expose the unrestrained material appetite of Jews. In his defense, others have argued that he treated Jews and Judaism in metaphorical terms in this essay and, in fact, used the occasion to promote the emancipation of Jews in European society.

Resolving the question of his true motives is less important here than recognizing that Marx was repeating a commonplace trope in equating Jews and money, or Judaism and commerce. The exaggerated forms that it took in the twentieth century ranged from the conspiratorial claims of world financial domination in *The Protocols* to the depiction of Jews as exploitive "blood-suckers."

In antiquity, anti-Jewish writers typically focused on the bizarre religious practices and social aloofness of Jews. But an early hint may reside in the story in the Gospel of Matthew (21:12) in which Jesus chases out the money-changers positioned in the courtyards of the Second Temple; this scene was immortalized in a painting by the Renaissance artist El Greco in 1600. The association between Jews and money became more explicit in the Middle Ages, especially as Christian rulers and clerics tightened restrictions on money-lending among members of their religion, thereby opening up an opportunity for Jews to fill the void. What was often regarded as an essential function by political leaders could be and often was treated with anger by the Christian populace, which generated new stereotypes of Jewish behavior. Thus, the image of the greedy money-lender joined in the growing demonization of the Jew in medieval Christian popular culture. In a curious anticipation of the present day, the actual presence of Jews was not required to propagate the image. After all, the most notorious representation of this Jewish type may well be Shylock, Shakespeare's protagonist in the late-sixteenth-century play "The

Merchant of Venice." Shakespeare constructed his profile of the hard-driving Jewish money-lender—who went so far as to demand an actual pound of flesh from the borrower, Antonio—despite the fact that Jews had been expelled from England in 1290 and would not be readmitted until 1656. This profile was a leap of imagination based less on personal contact than on inherited assumptions about Jews.

That said, the association between Jews and money was not an invention out of whole cloth. Jews were highly visible in vocations based in finance in medieval and early modern times. They were drawn to lucrative albeit dangerous commercial activities such as money-lending, tax-farming, and liquor production from which they had not been excluded. They developed considerable expertise in these domains and used their family and broader social networks to expand the scale of their trade. On the basis of these features, the German sociologist Werner Sombart argued in 1911 that it was Jews, impatient with the pace of medieval commerce, who laid the foundations for the modern capitalist system. Undoubtedly Jewish economic agents, from the court Jews to large German or Sephardic Jewish banking families, played an important role in helping to build national and international financial institutions in early modern and modern times. That said, it would be a mistake to reduce the complex evolution of capitalism to the actions of a small cohort of wealthy Jewish bankers.

Herein lies the complexity of the phenomenon. In the modern age Jews continue to be prominently and even overly represented in the upper echelons of banking and finance throughout the developed world. Moreover, Jews have been attracted to some forms of commerce, and not others, because they were permitted or encouraged to enter those fields. By the twentieth century, the accrued commercial acumen of the Jews and the abandonment of some anti-Jewish restrictions yielded high rates of affluence in many countries.

9. The Nazi tabloid *Der Stürmer* (The Stormer), published from 1923 to 1945, regularly ran sensationalist headlines and grotesque caricatures that vilified Jews. The headline of this front page reads, "Who Is the Enemy?" and the bottom declares, "The Jews Are Our Misfortune," a common antisemitic phrase since the late nineteenth century. The cartoon depicts a greedy Jew exploiting a fallen Europe.

That does not mean that there is a gene that disposes Jews toward money or commerce. In fact, while accused by antisemites of attempting to exploit others for their material gain, Jews have been as likely, if not likelier, to be involved in progressive and radical political movements that challenge capitalism. Alternately cast as communist subverters, economic parasites, and greedy capitalists, they have suffered from the remarkable malleability of antisemitism. Versions of all of those images, for example, surfaced in Nazi propaganda attacks on Jews, especially in the infamous German newspaper *Der Stürmer* (published from 1923 to 1945), which published material on a weekly basis. They echoed Adolf Hitler's own opinion of Jews, as expressed in his semi-autobiographical *Mein Kampf* (My Struggle), from which his subordinates liberally borrowed in devising the Final Solution.

"The world's foremost problem"

One of the most recurrent images in the modern age has been the allegation of a Jewish ambition to achieve worldwide domination found in the *Protocols of the Elders of Zion*. Not surprisingly, this assertion preceded the *Protocols*, becoming a popular claim in the very era in which the term "antisemitism" was born. In 1879, the German journalist Wilhelm Marr founded a League of Antisemites with the intention of repelling the influence of Jews in public life. In Marr's view, Jews, who represented about 1 percent of the German population in his day, waged battle against the Western world and vanquished it.

The 1870s—the decade during which Marr developed his new doctrine—were marked by social and economic instability. The sequence of major events that followed the Franco-Prussian War—military triumph, political unification, and economic collapse—set Germans on edge. In this environment, Jews became a vulnerable target, even though they had by this point become deeply rooted in German language, culture, and national identity. But it was precisely this assimilation that concerned the new antisemites. German legal scholar Karl Eugen Duehring declared in 1881 that it was the baptized Jews who were the gravest threats, because they were able to gain access to all corners of society without inhibition and thus assert their hegemonic aims.

Claims such as this placed a stain of permanence on Jewish identity that could not be erased, casting further doubt on the ability of Jews to be loyal citizens. Anti-Jewish words could and did lead to action in the late nineteenth century. Jews were held responsible for the assassination of Tsar Alexander II (1881), prompting a wave of violent pogroms. And the accusation against Alfred Dreyfus in France in 1894 rendered all French Jews suspect in the eyes of the anti-Dreyfusards.

The United States was not immune to the frenzy and panic. In the early twentieth century, the Michigan industrialist Henry Ford seized upon the claim of Jewish world domination and made it a centerpiece of the newspaper he published from 1919 to 1927, the *Dearborn Independent*, which became the second most widely circulated newspaper in the United States at the time (aided by the distribution network of the Ford Motor Company). Ford drew heavily on the *Protocols of the Elders of Zion* in the newspaper, fueling a mean streak of xenophobia throughout the country. He also collected a number of articles from the paper into a multivolume series that railed against Jews, the first book of which was titled *The International Jew: The World's Foremost Problem* (1920). Although Ford was forced to issue a public apology in 1927, the German government granted him a prestigious honor, the Grand Cross of the Eagle, in 1938. In fact, Adolf Hitler was said to have gained inspiration from Ford, with whom he shared a fear of the global Jewish threat.

More than half a century after Hitler's attempted genocide of the Jewish people, the myth of Jewish world domination still lives on. A quick Internet search of "Jewish World Domination" yields

The Ford International Weekly

THE DEARBORN
INDEPENDENT

One Dollar   Dearborn, Michigan, September 11, 1920   Five Cents

Jewish History

Millerand: France's Arch-Militarist

Paul Tyner, whose work has appeared in The Dearborn Independent at frequent intervals during the past year, has written this interesting picture of the workings of French politics.

When the Mokis of the West Dance

This year the Mokis dance! And palefaces from far and near throng to the desert land of the West to witness the survival of this strange aboriginal custom—the snake dancing to bring rain and good crops.

Will Clothing Price Tags Go Up or Down?

This is the second of two authoritative articles obtained by a staff writer for The Dearborn Independent. The price of men's and women's clothing is discussed as is the reason for the fluctuations.

Jewish Control of the American Press

Another of the series which discusses "The World's Foremost Problem, the International Jew," the most talked-of magazine feature in the country today.

Waving the Yellow Flag in California

You who have read the first of Mr. Wallace's two articles on the Japanese question on the Pacific Coast will need no urging to go on with the writer to the end of these informative and unbiased stories.

NEXT WEEK ALASKA NEXT WEEK

The most comprehensive article that has been written on Alaska and the tragedy that is taking place in that Far North territory will be begun in The Dearborn Independent next week. It will continue through several issues and the whole forms one of the most terrific arraignments of bureaucratic rule ever penned.

Thousands who went to Alaska to carve a home from the wilderness have left, broken by the exactions of the government which, it is charged, has shown little knowledge or consideration of the country's needs. This is the first time that the story has been told.

more than 500,000 results, reflecting a loose and unruly alliance of far-right conspiracy groups, neo-Nazis, and Muslim politicians.

The burdens and benefits of exceptionalism

The record of assailing, stigmatizing, and inflicting violence on Jews has been called the "longest hatred." Enduring for millennia and assuming multiple and often contradictory forms, the project of Jew-hatred has not only been about Jews. It also has lent a sense of coherence and purpose to societies the world over. Jews have been repeatedly cast as aliens, serving as a mirror onto the host society's own sense of self and collective insecurities.

The mirroring effect has been two way, since Jews have also reshaped and reinforced their sense of self in response to the stigma of the Gentile. In fact, antisemitism, up to a certain limit, has been a regular, if ironic, force of preservation for Jews. The tipping point comes when anti-Jewish expression reaches the precipice of murderous violence, at which point the preservative effects disappear.

And yet, as pervasive as antisemitism has been, it is important to emphasize again that it has not been the only factor defining relations between Jews and non-Jews. It is not simply that Jews have managed to live peaceably, if not always happily, next to their Gentile neighbors. It is not simply that they have absorbed the language, culture, and habits of the host societies, while sharing with those societies their own cultural proclivities. It is also that non-Jews

10. **The American industrialist Henry Ford, best known for his role in developing the Model T automobile, published the *Dearborn Independent*, which became a mass-circulation newspaper in the 1920s filled with antisemitic and xenophobic articles. The main article in the September 11, 1920, edition focused on alleged Jewish control of the press, which was part of a series later published as a book under the title *The International Jew: The World's Foremost Problem.***

have manifested "philosemitic" attitudes toward Jews, based on a healthy, and at times exaggerated, appreciation of their virtues.

This is a familiar phenomenon in the modern age. Nineteenth-century Christian Zionists in England and present-day Evangelical Christians in the United States have professed love for Jews because of their shared connection to the Holy Land. In the Asian world, a noticeable and growing body of literature is devoted to the Jews that speaks of their veneration for education and business. One popular Chinese writer, for example, calls the Jews "the most intelligent, mysterious, and the wealthiest people in the world." This adulation can at times linger at the border between respect and dangerous caricature, especially when addressing the Jews' financial success and global influence. But it is important to acknowledge that many people in the world today declare their affection and admiration, rather than contempt and hate, for Jews.

And this is not a product only of more recent times. When he heard of the expulsion of the Jews from Spain, the Ottoman sultan Bayezid II was said to have asked of his Spanish colleague: "How can you consider King Ferdinand a wise ruler when he impoverished his own land and enriched ours?"

Bayezid believed that Jews would be a force for good in his realm, chiefly for the usual reasons of their economic utility. On rare occasion, the appreciation extended beyond utility. One fascinating early case arose in the heart of medieval Christian Europe in 1235, when the Jews of the German town of Fulda were accused of the blood libel. Fulda was under the control of Frederick II, the polyglot Holy Roman Emperor whom the late nineteenth-century Swiss historian Jacob Burchkhardt called the first modern ruler. Upon hearing news of the libel, he set up a commission of inquiry to investigate the matter. When the first commission could not deliver a clear judgment, he convened a second commission that fully exonerated the Jews in 1236. In his letter of refutation, Frederick II not only affirmed the right to "security and peaceful status of the Jews of Germany," but also placed the Jews under his personal jurisdiction as servants of the court. Furthermore, Frederick dismissed out of hand the proposition that Jews would murder Christian children to use their blood. "Precisely the opposite," he clarified, "they guard against the intake of all blood, as we find expressly in the biblical book which is called in Hebrew, '*Bereshit*' [Genesis], in the laws given by Moses and in the Jewish decrees which are called in Hebrew, 'Talmud.'"

This effort to understand and evince sympathy for the beliefs and practices of Jews, in the face of considerable opposing pressure, makes Frederick's statement an interesting exception among medieval Christian rulers. Many of them formally tolerated Jews in their midst, but they did so solely on the grounds of their utility. It was not until the late eighteenth century that a more enduring shift in the nature of debates about Jews occurred. An important trailblazer was Christian Wilhelm Dohm, the Prussian legal scholar and friend of Moses Mendelssohn, who contemplated the rights and responsibilities of citizens at a crucial moment of change in European life. In 1781, Dohm wrote an essay titled "On the Amelioration of the Civil Status of the Jews" in which he averred that there was nothing in Judaism to prevent a Jew from "being a good citizen, if only the government will give him a citizen's rights." At the same time, Dohm was a product of his time inasmuch as he conceded that "the Jews may be more morally corrupt than other nations." But, and here appears the Enlightenment social engineer in Dohm, he continued: "this supposed greater moral corruption of the Jews is a necessary and natural consequence of the oppressed conditions in which they have been living for so many centuries." The presumed corruption of the Jews would disappear if they were liberated from externally imposed burdens.

Nearly a decade later, in August 1790, President George Washington followed up a visit to the Jewish community of Newport, Rhode Island, with a letter that discarded the old conditional language of toleration and replaced it with a grander vision of equality. Washington concluded with the hope that "the children of the stock of Abraham who dwell in this land continue to merit and enjoy the good will of the other inhabitants—while every one shall sit in safety under his own vine and fig tree and there shall be none to make him afraid."

To a great extent, Jews have realized the promise of Washington's America. They have been much admired, in no small part because of the belief that they are the progenitors of the biblical spirit on which America was built. It was this recognition that prompted Washington's successor, John Adams, to declare of the Jews in 1808: "They are the most glorious nation that ever inhabited this Earth."

Jews have also been admired because of their deep commitment to education, self-improvement, group cohesion, and assistance to others. Of course, that admiration is not universally held. The United States has had its share of xenophobic and antisemitic agitators, including Henry Ford and his fellow Michigander, the vitriolic radio preacher Father Charles Coughlin. And yet, the Jewish experience in the United States is unprecedented in terms of the freedom, degree of integration, and affluence that Jews have achieved. Whereas serious barriers prevented Jews as recently as the 1960s from gaining unfettered access to universities, business opportunities, social clubs, and political office in the United States, these restrictions have almost all vanished. No longer hobbled by social constraints of old, Jews in America seem to be inhabiting a Golden Age with few parallels in their long history. In fact, they were the most admired religious group in America in a 2014 survey by the Pew Research Center, a remarkable development in light of the history of the idea of the Jew in Gentile eyes.

Two countervailing scenarios can unravel this Golden Age. One is the previously theoretical question of how Jews would survive in a society devoid of antisemitism. Never having confronted it before, it is not clear how they would fare without the negative reinforcement of Jew-hatred, which has been a consistent and consistently preservative force. Especially in the modern period, when traditional forms of Jewish identity rooted in faith and ritual practice have waned somewhat or greatly, antisemitism has often served as a source of cohesion for Jews. Indeed, many Jews have defined and continue to define their identity in terms akin to Sigmund Freud, who, only when he encountered antisemites at the University of Vienna, "was made familiar with the fate of being in the Opposition."

And yet, the prospect that antisemitism will no longer be a preservative force—because it has been altogether eradicated—is premature. Anti-Jewish expression is following a pattern of historic decline in America, tempered somewhat by the new visibility of the "alt-right," with its mix of white nationalism and Nazi sympathizing. But the same cannot be said for the rest of the world. The other major center of Jewish life, the State of Israel, was conceived as a safe haven against antisemitism. It has developed a strong military that defends its citizens and, to an extent, Jews around the world. But Israel also stands at the center of a whirling and worsening conflict with the Palestinians that has fanned the flames of antisemitism in various parts of the world. Especially striking is its recurrence in Europe seventy years after the end of the Second World War.

In the face of the seeming decline of antisemitism in one key setting and rising rates in others, Jews again face challenges. From their two main centers, North America and Israel, and in smaller communities around the world, they will need to draw on all of their rich historical experience to make their way in the twenty-first century. That they have not only survived, but also flourished for millennia—prompting Winston Churchill to call them "the most formidable and the most remarkable race that has ever appeared in the world"—is the result of an uncanny ability to navigate between the poles of assimilation and antisemitism.

References

Introduction

"Ask the Rabbi": http://www.chabad.org/library/article_cdo/ aid/590597/jewish/How-and-why-have-Jews-survived-through- the-ages.htm.

"everlasting covenant": Genesis 17:7.

"netsah Yisra'el": The term, which refers to the eternity as well as victory of Israel, appears in the First Book of Samuel 15:29; it was also the name of a book by the early modern Prague scholar, Rabbi Judah Loew, known as the MaHaRaL.

"Mercurians": The term is used by historian Yuri Slezkine as a contrast to land-based "Apollonians" in his important book *The Jewish Century* (Princeton, NJ: Princeton University Press, 2004).

"Secret of survival": This term was used by Simon Dubnow in a 1912 essay published in the Hebrew journal *He-`atid*, "Sod ha-kiyum," and translated in Koppel Pinson's edition of Simon Dubnow, *Nationalism and History* (Philadelphia: Jewish Publication Society, 1958), 333.

"Alliance of Jews with political sovereigns": This concept figured centrally in Hannah Arendt's discussion of antisemitism in *The Origins of Totalitarianism* (New York: Schocken, 1951), 23.

"'Gentile hatred' that preserved the Jews": Benedictus Spinoza used the term in his 1670 book, *A Politico-Theological Treatise*, translated by R. H. M. Elwes (London: G. Bell and Sons, 1883), 55.

"Lachrymose" view of Jewish history: The canonical phrase of Salo Baron appears in his essay, "Ghetto and Emancipation: Shall We Revise the Traditional View?" *The Menorah Journal* 14 (June 1928): 526.

"The usage of historian Gerson Cohen": See the idiosyncratic views of Cohen in "The Blessing of Assimilation in Jewish History," Commencement Address delivered at Hebrew College, Brookline, MA, 1966.

Chapter 1: Names

"What's in a name": William Shakespeare, "Romeo and Juliet" (1597).

"Gershom Scholem once declared": Scholem declared that "Judaism cannot be defined according to its essence, because it has no essence." See his entry "Judaism" in Arthur A. Cohen and Arnold Eisen, *Contemporary Jewish Religious Thought* (New York: Charles Scribner's Sons, 1987), 505.

"BCE": The terms BCE and CE stand for Before the Common Era and Common Era. They are considered more neutral and appropriate as terms of reference for Jewish history than BC—Before Christ—and AD—Anno Domini, the Year of the Lord, referring to the birth of Jesus Christ. Jews have traditionally counted time according to their own lunar-based calendar that had reached 5777 years in the year 2017.

"Israel is laid waste": https://en.wikipedia.org/wiki/Merneptah_Stele.

"Including, some suggest, the practice...": L. I. Rabinowitz raised the prospect that "(i)t is to the period of the Babylonian Exile that one must look for the origin of the synagogue." See "Synagogue," *Encyclopaedia Judaica* (Jerusalem: Keter, 1972), 15: 580. See also Lee Levine, *The Ancient Synagogue: The First Thousand Years*, 2nd ed. (New Haven, CT: Yale University Press, 2005), 25.

"Portable fatherland": Heinrich Heine, "Confessions," *The Prose Writings of Heinrich Heine*, introduced by Havelock Ellis (London: Walter Scott, 1887), http://www.gutenberg.org/files/37478/37478-h/37478-h.htm.

"This literacy offered Jews, it has been argued, a competitive advantage": This claim anchors the recent book by Maristella Botticini and Zvi Eckstein, *The Chosen Few: How Education Shaped Jewish History, 70–1492* (Princeton, NJ: Princeton University Press, 2012). For a divergent view, see Catherine Hezser, *Jewish Literacy in Roman Palestine* (Tübingen, Germany: Mohr Siebeck, 2001).

"Ahl al-Kitāb" (People of the Book): http://www.britannica.com/topic/Ahl-al-Kitab.

"Women appeared in courts to represent their interests as frequently as men." This account relies on the *Geniza* materials brilliantly analyzed by S. D. Goitein, *A Mediterranean Society*, vol. 3, *The Family* (Berkeley: University of California Press, 1978), 336.

"My heart is in the East and I am at the edge of the West": T. Carmi, ed. *The Penguin Book of Hebrew Verse* (New York: Viking, 1981), 347.

"All Israel are responsible for one another": Babylonian Talmud 39a.

"Great" or "holy nation" (Goy): (Gen. 12:2, Ex. 19:6).

"Rebel leader in Yemen decreed compulsory apostasy for the Jews": From Maimonides, "Epistle to Yemen," in *Crisis and Leadership: Epistles of Maimonides*, ed. David Hartman (Philadelphia: The Jewish Publication Society of America, 1985), 95.

"A new and revitalizing spirit": Nachman Krochmal, *More nevukhe ha-zeman* included in Simon Rawidowicz, ed., *Kitve RaNaK*, 40. See also Jay M. Harris, *Nachman Krochmal: Guiding the Perplexed of the Modern Age* (New York: New York University Press, 1993), 126–55.

"Pew Research Center": "A Portrait of Jewish Americans," http://www .pewforum.org/2013/10/01/jewish-american-beliefs-attitudes-culture-survey/ (New York: Schocken, 1967), 17.

Chapter 2: Numbers

"Some 14 million Jews": "Projected Changes in Global Jewish Population," http://www.pewforum.org/2015/04/02/jews/.

"About six hundred thousand (Israelite) men": Exodus 12: 37.

"Or was more of an aspirational dream of rabbis": For a skeptical view of the existence of an actual Sanhedrin, see David M. Goodblatt, *The Monarchic Principle: Studies in Jewish Self-Government in Antiquity* (Tübingen, Germany: Mohr Siebeck, 1994), 105ff.

"The decline, which may have reduced the Jewish population from 4.5 million to one million people...": Sergio DellaPergola, "Some Fundamentals of Jewish Demographic History," in S. DellaPergola and J. Even, *Papers in Jewish Demography* (Jerusalem: Hebrew University, 1997), 11–33.

"A more recent estimate...": "Genes Suggest Woman at Root of Ashkenazi Family Tree," October 8, 2013, *New York Times*, http:// www.nytimes.com/2013/10/09/science/ashkenazi-origins-may-be-with-european-women-study-finds.html.

"There were 40,000 Jews": Benjamin of Tudela, *The Itinerary of Benjamin of Tudela: Critical Text, Translation and Commentary*, ed. Marcus Nathan Adler (New York: Phillip Feldheim, 1907), https://depts.washington.edu/silkroad/texts/tudela.html.

"Among the qualities that define the age": The historian David Ruderman has enumerated these qualities in his *Early Modern Jewry: A Cultural History* (Princeton, NJ: Princeton University Press, 2010), 14–15.

"Ticket of admission": Heinrich Heine (c. 1823), included in Mendes-Flohr and Reinharz, *The Jew in the Modern World*, 806.

"The conventionally assumed trigger point…" A number of historians have questioned whether 1881 was such a trigger point. See Benjamin Nathans, *Beyond the Pale: The Jewish Encounter with Late Imperial Russia* (Berkeley: University of California Press, 2002), 8.

"189,000 Holocaust survivors in Israel": Quoted in "Thousands of Holocaust Survivors Still Living in Poverty, Fighting for Recognition," *Haaretz*, April 13, 2015.

Chapter 3: Cultures

"All lands are as dough…": Babylonian Talmud Kiddushin 69b.

"If a Portuguese Jew in England…": Isaac de Pinto, *Apologie pour la nation juive* (1762), quoted in Paul Mendes-Flohr and Jehuda Reinharz, eds. *The Jew in the Modern World: A Documentary History*, 3rd ed. (New York: Oxford University Press, 2011), 280–82.

"Monolatry": http://www.britannica.com/topic/monolatry.

"Shalem, a word that connotes…": The term was used by the early Hungarian *haredi* activist Akiva Yosef Schlesinger. See the entry on Schlesinger in the *YIVO Encyclopedia of Jews in Eastern Europe*, accessed at http://www.yivoencyclopedia.org/article.aspx/ Schlesinger_Akiva_Yosef.

"Born of the same parent…": On the view that early Christianity and rabbinic Judaism should be regarded as siblings, see Alan F. Segal, *Rebecca's Children: Judaism and Christianity in the Roman World* (Cambridge, MA: Harvard University Press, 1986), and Israel Jacob Yuval, *Two Nations in Your Womb: Perception of Jews and Christians in Late Antiquity and the Middle Ages* (Berkeley: University of California Press, 2006).

"A single circulatory system": Daniel Boyarin, *Dying for God: Martyrdom and the Making of Judaism and Christianity* (Stanford, CA: Stanford University Press, 1999), 9.

"Give me Yavneh and her sages": Babylonian Talmud Gittin 56b.

"Over and over again": Ben Bag-Bag is quoted as saying in Pirke Avot 5:22: "Turn it, and turn it, for everything is in it."

"The Geniza was the repository...": The scholar who made most
   wide-ranging use of the Geniza materials was Goitein in his
   five-volume masterpiece *A Mediterranean Society*.

"Horrible heresies": From the language of the writ of excommunication against Spinoza from the Mahamad of the Amsterdam Jewish
   community in Mendes-Flohr and Reinharz, *The Jew in the Modern
   World*, 62.

"Radical Enlightenment": See Jonathan I. Israel, *The Radical
   Enlightenment: Philosophy and the Making of Modernity,
   1650–1750* (Oxford: Oxford University Press, 2001).

"Neutral society": The historian Jacob Katz pioneered use of the term
   in his *Tradition and Crisis: Jewish Society at the End of the Middle
   Ages* (New York: Free Press, 1961).

"Dry baptism": Amos Elon, *The Pity of It All: A Portrait of the German-
   Jewish Epoch, 1743–1933* (New York: Henry Holt, 2002), 203.

"Seemed to me the greatest shame": Rahel Varnhagen's supposed
   death-bed confession is quoted in Elon, *The Pity of It All*, 89–90.

Chapter 4: Politics

"One must refuse everything...": Count Clermont-Tonnerre's statement
   from December 23, 1789, in the French National Assembly in
   Mendes-Flohr and Reinharz, *The Jew in the Modern World*, 124.

"Auto-emancipation": This is the title of Dr. Leo Pinsker's pamphlet, in
   which the term "Judeophobia" appears. Pinsker, *Auto-Emancipation*,
   translated by D. S. Blondheim (New York: Maccabean Publishing,
   1906).

"St. Augustine developed his view...": Augustine's view of the Jews
   as "witnesses" can be found in *Contra Judaeos*, http://www2
   .pugetsound.edu/faculty/tinsley/Courses/hum303/AJAugustine.
   htm. See also Stephan R. Hayes, *Reluctant Witnesses: Jews and the
   Christian Imagination* (Louisville, KY: Westminister John Knox
   Press, 1995), 28.

"Ought to suffer no prejudice": "The Letters of Pope Gregory I,"
   Church Quarterly Review 12 (1881): 156.

"Vertical" or "royal alliance": The historian Yosef Hayim Yerushalmi
   has given a compelling account of the Jews' "royal alliance" in *The
   Lisbon Massacre of 1506 and the Royal Image in the "Shebet
   Yehudah"* (Cincinnati: Hebrew Union College, 1976). See also Lois
   C. Dubin, "Yosef Hayim Yerushalmi, the Royal Alliance, and Jewish
   Political Theory," *Jewish History* 28 (2014): 51–81.

"Hannah Arendt questioned whether": Arendt's criticism of Jewish political behavior, especially of the local Jewish councils (Judenräte), is found in her *Eichmann in Jerusalem: A Report on the Banality of Evil* (New York: Viking Press, 1963).

"Nation within a nation": The phrase is used, for example, by Count Clermont-Tonnerre in his speech to the French National Assembly from December 23, 1789, on the question of granting Jews rights of citizenship; an English translation is in Mendes-Flohr and Reinharz, *The Jew in the Modern World*, 124. See also the article by Jacob Katz, "A State within a State: The History of an Anti-Semitic Slogan," in idem, *Emancipation and Assimilation: Studies in Modern Jewish History* (Farnborough, UK: Gregg International, 1972), 47–76.

"Justice, justice, thou shall pursue:" Deuteronomy 16: 20.

"Prepared the way for a new era": Selma Stern, *The Court Jew: A Contribution to the History of the Period of Absolutism in Europe*, translated by Ralph Weiman (Philadelphia: Jewish Publication Society, 1950), 267.

"Divest ourselves entirely...": Berr Isaac Berr's statement in a letter from 1791 is in Mendes-Flohr and Reinharz, *The Jew in the Modern World*, 129.

"Sovereign self": The term anchors the analysis of Steven M. Cohen and Arnold M. Eisen, *Self, Family, and Community in America* (Bloomington: Indiana University Press, 2000), 13–42.

Chapter 5: Perceptions

"Jean-François Lyotard juxtaposed real-life Jews to 'jews'": Jean-François Lyotard, *Heidegger and "the jews"* (Minneapolis: University of Minnesota Press, 1990).

"Universal hate": Spinoza, *A Theologico-Political Treatise*, 55.

"I decide who is a Jew": Karl Lueger, *I Decide Who Is a Jew: The Papers of Karl Lueger*, ed. Richard Geehr (Lanham, MD: University Press of America, 1982).

"The stranger, the intruder...": Jean-Paul Sartre, *Anti-Semite and Jew*, translated by George J. Becker (New York: Schocken, 1995), 83.

"The Anti-Defamation League global survey": L Global 100, http://global100.adl.org/.

"A Portrait of Jewish Americans": Pew Research Center, October 1, 2013, http://www.pewforum.org/2013/10/01/jewish-american-beliefs-attitudes-culture-survey/.

"A novel form of worship...": Tacitus, *The Histories*, Book 5, #4, http://classics.mit.edu/Tacitus/histories.5.v.html.

"Bloodsuckers who attack the Palestinians": "Morsi's Slurs against Jews Stir Concern," *New York Times*, January 14, 2013.

"History's most bloodthirsty people": The article "Who are history's most bloodthirsty people?" appeared on the website of Iranian parliamentarian Ahmad Tavakkoli. It is discussed by Mehdi Khalaji in "The Classic Blood Libel Goes Mainstream in Iran," April 21, 2015, http://www.washingtoninstitute.org/policy-analysis/view/the-classic-blood-libel-against-jews-goes-mainstream-in-iran.

"You are wicked deceivers...": Louis Farrakhan speech from February 25, 1996, https://www.splcenter.org/fighting-hate/extremist-files/individual/louis-farrakhan.

"Money is the jealous God of Israel": Karl Marx, "On the Jewish Question," *The Marx-Engels Reader*, edited by Robert C. Tucker, http://genius.com/Robert-c-tucker-the-marx-engels-reader-chapter-16-on-the-jewish-question-annotated.

"The Merchant of Venice": William Shakespeare, *The Merchant of Venice* (1596–1598).

"Werner Sombart argued in 1911": Werner Sombart's 1911 book, *Die Juden und das Wirtschaftsleben*, was published as *The Jews and Modern Capitalism*, translated by M. Epstein (New York: E. P. Dutton, 1913).

"The world's foremost problem": Henry Ford, *The International Jew: The World's Foremost Problem* (Dearborn, MI: Dearborn Publishing, 1920).

"Have waged battle...": Wilhelm Marr made this observation in an 1879 book *Der Sieg des Judenthums über das Germanenthum*, excerpted in Mendes-Flohr and Reinharz, *The Jew in the Modern World*, 306.

"It was the Jews who had been baptized...": Karl Eugen Duehring's claim comes in his book *Die Judenfrage also Racen- Sitten- und Culturfrage* (1881), excerpted in Mendes-Flohr and Reinharz, *The Jew in the Modern World*, 308.

"Longest hatred": Robert Wistrich, *Antisemitism: The Longest Hatred* (London: Thames Methuen, 1991).

"Present-day Evangelical Christians": See Yaakov Ariel, *An Unusual Relationship: Evangelical Christians and the Jews* (New York: New York University Press, 2013).

"A noticeable and growing body of literature...": On Jews as a source of interest and respect in China, see James Ross, "China's Search for the Secret of Jewish Success," *Tablet*, January 25, 2016. Accessed at

http://www.tabletmag.com/jewish-life-and-religion/196382/
chinas-secrets-of-jewish-success. On Japanese fascination with
Jews, see David G. Goodman and Masanori Miyazawa, *Jews in the
Japanese Mind: The History and Use of a Cultural Stereotype*
(New York: Free Press, 1995).

"How can you consider King Ferdinand…": Israel Zinberg: *A History
of Jewish Literature: The Jewish Center of Culture in the Ottoman
Empire*, translated by Bernard Martin (New York: Ktav Publishing,
1974), 17.

"Security and peaceful status of the Jews of Germany" and "Precisely
the opposite": Frederick II's letter of 1236 is found at http://
www.ccjr.us/dialogika-resources/primary-texts-from-the-history-of
-the-relationship/265-frederick-ii.

"From being a good citizen" and "may be more morally corrupt":
C. W. Dohm's 1781 essay, "On the Amelioration of the Civil Status
of the Jews," is excerpted in Mendes-Flohr and Reinharz, *The Jew
in the Modern World*, 29.

"The children of the stock of Abraham": President George
Washington's letter of 21 August 1790 can be found at http://www
.tourosynagogue.org/history-learning/gw-letter.

"They are the most glorious nation…" The quote from President John
Adam's letter of 1808 can be found in Abraham P. Bloch, *One Day:
An Anthology of Jewish Historical Anniversaries for Every Day of
the Year* (New York: Ktav, 1987), 367.

"The most admired religious group in America in a 2014 survey by the
Pew Research Center": "How Americans Feel about Religious
Groups," Pew Research Center, 16 July 2014. Accessed at http://
www.pewforum.org/2014/07/16/
how-americans-feel-about-religious-groups/.

"Fate of being in the Opposition": Sigmund Freud's reflections,
originally published in 1925, appear in *An Autobiographical Study*,
translated by James Strachey (New York and London: W. W.
Norton and Company, 1952), 7.

"The most formidable and the most remarkable": Winston Churchill,
"Zionism versus Bolshevism," *The Illustrated Sunday Herald*
(London), 8 February 1920.

Further reading

Arendt, Hannah. *Rahel Varnhagen: The Life of a Jewess.* Baltimore: Johns Hopkins University Press, 1997.

Arendt, Hannah. *The Origins of Totalitarianism.* New York: Schocken, 1951.

Baer, Yitzhak F. *Galut.* New York: Schocken, 1947.

Barnavi, Eli. *A Historical Atlas of the Jewish People from the Time of the Patriarchs to the Present.* New York: Schocken, 1992.

Baron, Salo. *A Social and Religious History of the Jews.* 2nd rev. ed. New York: Columbia University Press/Jewish Publication Society, 1952.

Ben-Sasson, H. H., ed. *A History of the Jewish People.* Cambridge, MA: Harvard University Press, 1985.

Biale, David, ed. *Cultures of the Jews: A New History.* New York: Schocken, 2002.

Biale, David. *Power and Powerlessness in Jewish History.* New York: Schocken, 1986.

Boyarin, Jonathan, and Daniel Boyarin. *Powers of Diaspora: Two Essays on the Relevance of Jewish Culture.* Minneapolis: University of Minnesota Press, 1997.

Brody, Robert. *The Geonim of Babylonia and the Shaping of Medieval Jewish Culture.* New Haven, CT: Yale University Press, 1998.

Chabon, Michaael. *The Yiddish Policemen's Union.* New York: HarperCollins, 2007.

Cohen, Julia Phillips, and Sarah Abrevaya Stein. *Sephardi Lives: A Documentary History, 1700–1950.* Stanford, CA: Stanford University Press, 2015.

Cohen, Shaye J. D. *The Beginnings of Jewishness: Boundaries, Varieties, Uncertainties.* Berkeley: University of California Press, 2001.

Efron, John. *Defenders of the Race: Jewish Doctors and Race Science in Fin-de-siècle Europe*. New Haven, CT: Yale University Press, 1994.

Elon, Amos. *The Pity of It All: A Portrait of the German-Jewish Epoch, 1743–1933*. New York: Henry Holt, 2002.

Fleming, K. E. *Greece: A Jewish History*. Princeton, NJ: Princeton University Press, 2008.

Frederiksen, Paula. *Augustine and the Jews: A Christian Defense of Jews and Judaism*. New Haven, CT: Yale University Press, 2010.

Friedländer, Saul. *Nazi Germany and the Jews*. Vol. 1, *The Years of Persecution, 1933–1939*. New York: HarperCollins, 1997.

Friedländer, Saul. *The Years of Extermination: Nazi Germany and the Jews, 1939–1945*. New York: HarperCollins, 2007.

Funkenstein, Amos. *Perceptions of Jewish History*. Berkeley: University of California Press, 1993.

Gruen, Erich. *Heritage and Hellenism: The Reinvention of Jewish Tradition*. Berkeley: University of California Press, 1998.

Halbertal, Moshe. *Maimonides: Life and Thought*. Princeton, NJ: Princeton University Press, 2013.

Harshav, Benjamin. *Language in Time of Revolution*. Stanford, CA: Stanford University Press, 1999.

Hertzberg, Arthur, ed. *The Zionist Idea: A Historical Analysis and Reader*. Philadelphia: Jewish Publication Society, 1997.

Herzl, Theodor. *The Jewish State*. Translated by Harry Zohn. New York: Herzl Press, 1970.

Hoffman, Adina, and Peter Cole. *Sacred Trash: The Lost and Found World of the Cairo Geniza*. New York: Schocken, 2011.

Karlip, Joshua. *The Tragedy of a Generation: The Rise and Fall of Jewish Nationalism in Eastern Europe*. Cambridge, MA: Harvard University Press, 2013.

Katz, Jacob. *From Prejudice to Destruction: Anti-Semitism, 1700–1933*. Cambridge, MA: Harvard University Press, 1980.

Katznelson, Ira, and Pierre Birnbaum, eds. *Paths of Emancipation: Jews, States, and Citizenship*. Princeton, NJ: Princeton University Press, 2014.

Langmuir, Gavin. *Toward a Definition of Antisemitism*. Berkeley: University of California Press, 1990.

Livak, Olga. *Haskalah: The Romantic Movement in Judaism*. New Brunswick, NJ: Rutgers University Press, 2012.

Mendelsohn, Ezra. *On Modern Jewish Politics*. New York: Oxford University Press, 1993.

Mendelssohn, Moses. *Jerusalem: Or on Religious Power and Judaism.* Translated by Allan Arkush. Waltham, MA: Brandeis University Press, 1983.

Mendes-Flohr, Paul, and Jehuda Reinharz. *The Jew in the Modern World: A Documentary History.* 3rd ed. New York: Oxford University Press, 2011.

Nirenberg, David. *Anti-Judaism: The Western Tradition.* New York: W. W. Norton, 2013.

Ostrer, Harry. *Legacy: A Genetic History of the Jewish People.* Oxford: Oxford University Press, 2012.

Penslar, Derek Jonathan. *Shylock's Children: Economics and Jewish Identity in Modern Europe.* Berkeley: University of California Press, 2001.

Pianko, Noam. *Jewish Peoplehood: An American Innovation.* New Brunswick, NJ: Rutgers University Press, 2015.

Rabinovitch, Simon, ed. *Jews and Diaspora Nationalism: Writings on Jewish Peoplehood in Europe and the United States.* Waltham, MA: Brandeis University Press, 2012.

Roth, Cecil. *Doña Gracia of the House of Nasi.* Philadelphia: Jewish Publication Society, 2009.

Roth, Philip. *Operation Shylock: A Confession.* New York: Simon and Schuster, 1993.

Ruderman, David. *Early Modern Jewry: A New Cultural History.* Princeton, NJ: Princeton University Press, 2011.

Ruppin, Arthur. *The Jews of Today.* London: G. Bell and Sons, 1913.

Sartre, Jean-Paul. *Anti-Semite and Jew: An Exploration of the Etiology of Hate.* New York: Schocken, 1948.

Schaefer, Peter. *The History of the Jews in Antiquity: The Jews of Palestine from Alexander the Great to the Arab Conquest.* New York: Routledge, 1995.

Schniedewind, William. *A Social History of Hebrew: Its Origins through the Rabbinic Period.* New Haven, CT: Yale University Press, 2013.

Slezkine, Yuri. *The Jewish Century.* Princeton, NJ: Princeton University Press, 2006.

Smith, Mark S. *The Origins of Biblical Monotheism: Israel's Polytheistic Background and the Ugaritic Texts.* Oxford: Oxford University Press, 2001.

Stern, Selma. *The Court Jew: A Contribution to the History of Absolutism in Europe.* Translated by Ralph Weiman. Philadelphia: Jewish Publication Society, 1950.

Walzer, Michael, Menachem Lorberbaum, and Noam J. Zohar, eds. *The Jewish Political Tradition.* Vol. 1, *Authority.* New Haven, CT: Yale University Press, 2000–2006.

Wexler, Paul. *The Ashkenazic Jews: A Slavo-Turkic People in Search of a Jewish Identity.* Bloomington, IN: Slavica, 1993.

Yerushalmi, Yosef Hayim. *From Spanish Court to Italian Ghetto: Isaac Cardoso; A Study in Seventeenth-Century Marranism and Jewish Apologetics.* New York: Columbia University Press, 1971.

Yerushalmi, Yosef Hayim. *Zakhor: Jewish History and Jewish Memory.* Seattle: University of Washington Press, 1982.

Yuval, Israel Jacob. *Two Nations in Your Womb: Perceptions of Jews and Christians in Late Antiquity and the Middle Ages.* Translated by Barbara Harshav and Jonathan Chipman. Berkeley: University of California Press, 2006.

Jewish History

Index

Index